Praise for *Sacred America*

genocide of Indigenous Peoples, as well as honoring their unique and invaluable contributions to our collective future."

—Hereditary Chief Phil Lane Jr., member of the Dakota and
Chickasaw Nation; global trustee, United Religions Initiative; and
chairman of the Four Worlds International Institute

"If, as the Bible says, 'where there is no vision, the people perish,' then this book is our survival manual. It provides exactly the vision we, the people, have been searching for."

—Mark Gerzon, author of *Leading Through Conflict* and *The Reunited States of America*

"This is the first great manifesto of the evolutionary, trans-partisan political movement of our time. . . . In this appealingly personal but deeply knowledgeable book, Stephen Dinan shows us a better way. Like some of the great political philosophers of the 19th century, he shines a spotlight on the most promising currents of the day. . . . He shows us how we can better become the richly complex and self-aware beings that we truly are."

—Mark Satin, author of *New Age Politics* and *Radical Middle*

"Bookstores are full of attempts to map the transition from the last century into the new one and away from a world full of silos, hard-edged ideologies, and personal agendas. Dinan's vision is unique. He is recognized as the prime 'shift-master' of our age and generation because he goes where most fear to tread and maps out new and fresh blends of tools and alloys that hold the promise of creating a brighter day for all. Get a copy of *Sacred America, Sacred World*. No! Buy 10 and delight your friends."

—Don Edward Beck, PhD, Center for Human Emergence, Denton, Texas

"This is an important book and does a great job at connecting the big issues of our day, making it real and compelling for readers to act in ways that speak to the 'better angels of our nature.'"

—Diane Randall, executive secretary of Friends Committee on National Legislation

"Dinan's book is a shot across the bow of political complacency. He is calling on Americans from across the political spectrum to aspire to something higher than the conventional ideas and institutions that now drive our politics. He points to the reality of order and freedom as energetic forces within individuals and the culture as well as the need to address the country's psychic shadow. It's a starting point for very important conversations that must take place if our constitutional republic is to not only survive but thrive."

—Michael D. Ostrolenk, transpartisan social entrepreneur;
cofounder of the Liberty Coalition

"*Sacred America, Sacred World* provides a valuable voyager's guide to traversing the uncharted waters of planetary transformation. It points us in the direction of functional transpartisan politics, sustainable economics, and our individual responsibility as participants in nurturing civilization's evolution. The insights offered in this powerful book have the potential to change the world."

—Bruce H. Lipton, PhD, bestselling author of *The Biology of Belief*

"Very few times in one's life does a book of monumental importance and significance come along. This book is one of those times. *Sacred America, Sacred World* will awaken the deep dream within you for the next level of the expression of America's soul in the world. Stephen both honors ideologies and also transcends them into a shared mission and destiny for America and humanity. This book is nothing less than the blueprint and the foundation for the next level of the American Dream."

—Martin Rutte, bestselling author of *Chicken Soup for the Soul at Work*

"Reading Stephen Dinan's epic tome during a presidential election year full of debased debates is like opening a window to a room that's been hermetically sealed for decades. This book is disruptively sacred, delectably stimulating, and deeply spiritual. Read it and reap."

—Chip Conley, bestselling author of *Peak*, entrepreneur who built a $250M business, top-rated TED presenter

"This wise and moving book will help us all in the central task of our time. That of reinventing a way of being and doing that reflects our sacred nature and sacred purpose."

—Andrew Harvey, author of over 30 books and founder of Institute for Sacred Activism

"Stephen Dinan has performed a unique feat: he has created a holistic view of the future of the United States without demonizing anyone. This book is a powerful road map to a better world and a better country. It will be a guide-book for visionaries, activists, and change agents for years to come."

—Tim Kelley, global consultant, author of *True Purpose*

"Responding to a broken political world of ends-justified tactics and narrow self-interests, Dinan provides a positive, holistic vision for our democracy."

—Don Ness, former mayor, Duluth, Minnesota

"Stephen Dinan invites us to connect with the sacred mission to reinvent the world that is America's deep reason for being. He provides us with many transformative strategies to do that, but underneath each of them is a being infused with hope for the future and an indomitable belief in possibility. Read this book if you wish to be infused with Stephen's two precious gifts for navigating the 21st century on Planet Earth."

—David Gershon, CEO of Empowerment Institute and author of
Social Change 2.0: A Blueprint for Reinventing the World

"*Sacred America, Sacred World* offers an inspiring vision of our spiritual roots and our future potential as a nation, while also addressing shadow elements that need healing. It provides fascinating insights on how to transcend rigid liberal/conservative ideologies, based on the author's own experience, and gives many useful ideas for how citizens can get engaged in transforming America."

—Corinne McLaughlin and Gordon Davidson, coauthors of *Spiritual Politics* and cofounders of The Center for Visionary Leadership

"Heartfelt and personal, yet also well-informed by leading-edge political thinking, I highly recommend this thoughtful and thoroughly readable book."

—Steve McIntosh, author of *Integral Consciousness and the Future of Evolution*

"Rarely does a book come along that not only presents an illuminating picture of how our country and our world can evolve to work for everyone, but also offers profound understanding about how to get there. *Sacred America, Sacred World* is such a book and a remarkable achievement. As we approach America's 250th anniversary, Stephen's pragmatic vision can excite and guide us. A deep bow to his intelligence, his heart, and his commitment to our beloved country and the world."

—John Steiner, co-founder, The Bridge Alliance, and
Margo King, Wisdom Beyond Borders

"The American Dream used to mean something. With the heartfelt inspiration and practical wisdom offered in Stephen's book, it can once again. Read this book if you are an advocate for not just rebuilding America but for truly making the world holy. *Sacred America, Sacred World* opens doorways and pathways into the world we have barely believed possible, and it is time now to make that dream real. In many ways, this powerful book is the answer to our prayers."

—Marcia Wieder, CEO of The Meaning Institute and bestselling author of *DREAM*

"I am sitting here crying and cannot begin to express how touched I was by everything you wrote and how proud I am of the person you have become and your vision for our country and world. It is the best book I have ever read!!"

—Mom

SACRED AMERICA
SACRED WORLD

Fulfilling Our Mission
in Service to All

Stephen Dinan

Foreword by Marianne Williamson

HAMPTON ROADS

Cover design by MettaGraphics
Cover photograph © MettaGraphics
Interior by Frame25 Productions
Typeset in Requiem Text

Hampton Roads Publishing Company, Inc.
Charlottesville, VA 22906
Distributed by Red Wheel/Weiser, LLC
www.redwheelweiser.com

Sign up for our newsletter and special offers by going to www.redwheelweiser.com/newsletter/.

ISBN: 978-1-57174-744-0

Library of Congress Cataloging-in-Publication Data

Names: Dinan, Stephen, 1970- author.
Title: Sacred America, sacred world : fulfilling our mission in service to all / Stephen Dinan ; foreword by Marianne Williamson.
Description: Charlottesville, VA : Hampton Roads Publishing, 2016.
| Includes
  bibliographical references.
Identifiers: LCCN 2016005259 | ISBN 9781571747440 (paperback)
Subjects: LCSH: United States--Social policy--2009- | United States--Economic policy--2009- | United States--Politics and govern-ment--2009- |
  Democracy--United States. | Democracy--Forecasting. | BISAC: POLITICAL
  SCIENCE / Public Policy / Cultural Policy. | POLITICAL SCI-ENCE /
  Government / International. | SOCIAL SCIENCE / Future Studies.
Classification: LCC HN59.2 .D56 2016 | DDC 306.0973--dc23
LC record available at

Printed in the United States of America

M&G

10 9 8 7 6 5 4 3 2 1

This book is dedicated to the ever-unfolding creativity of America, as well as all those who have labored to help our country shine with liberty and justice for all.

Contents

Foreword

The book in your hands is about vision. It is a conversation about a possible America, and by extension a possible world.

Visionary Werner Erhard once famously remarked that "you can live your life out of your circumstances, or you can live your life out of a vision." America's circumstances have never been more complicated than they are today, with elements ranging from the most innovative and promising to the most corrupt and disheartening. What we need is not simply more complicated analysis along the same lines of thinking that produced our circumstances as they are now. What we need is a vision of what's possible, and *Sacred America, Sacred World* pours thought and feeling into the envisioning process.

Dinan posits that this new envisioning is not just the work of our leaders, but of all citizens. Only when we find a new conversation, a new overriding vision to guide us, will we find the will and the way to make it manifest.

In reading this book, you will consider, along with the author, not just how things are but how they could be. You will join him in questioning the limitations as well as recognizing the higher principles of both the right and left. You will realize the power of the warrior archetype yet see the shadow of unprincipled power. You will see the value of the marketplace as well as the importance of ethics and social responsibility within it. You will recognize where America has deviated from our higher principles, and the blessings that have emerged when we have held to them. You will understand the importance of taking responsibility for our mistakes, as well as the healing that results when we dedicate ourselves to solutions. The author is a worthy guide to assuming our critical role as the dreamers of a new America.

According to Dinan, we need a movement of "evolutionaries" to midwife a new chapter in American history. He argues our need for a new operating system in our politics, media, and other major institutions, while staying focused on the internal changes out of which such a new system would spring forth. "Sacred citizenship," with its emphasis on the values of "oneness, respect, and love," is the only vessel powerful enough to both dissolve the darkness that has infected our nation and give birth to a redeemed America. Each of us can and must play our part, in our personal lives as well as in collaboration with politicians, if we are to usher in the higher possibilities for life on earth. In reading this book, we are participating mentally in an evolutionary process out of which will flow the re-greening of our nation. This is not just a calling of our citizenship; it is a calling of our souls.

One of the strongest elements in *Sacred America, Sacred World* is its call to spiritual seekers to focus attention on our collective lives as both American and global citizens. Herein lies tremendous potential for social good, as those with the deepest dedication to the realization of the Divine begin to apply such realization to social and political spheres. From citizen lobbying for the Friends Committee on National Legislation to support of Wolf PAC in its work on overturning Citizens United, Dinan traces his own political involvement from mainly *observing* the news on television to actively *participating* in trying to change it. Reading this book helps clarify some of the most important problems that face us now, helping to dissolve the web of obfuscation that keeps so many of them in place. Yet it is a roadmap as well, as Dinan envisions, among other things, a collective World Campaign 2020 in which we harness our dreams and activism in a climactic burst of energy and change.

Of Dinan, some may say that he's a dreamer; but in the words of John Lennon, "he's not the only one." Dinan is correct in pointing out the extraordinary power that lies latent in the hearts of so many in America and around the world who do want positive change, and who do want to feel they can play a part in making it happen. His helpfulness lies not only in celebrating this power but also in describing various ways it can be harnessed for practical results. Regardless of our politics, or whether we agree with every aspect of Dinan's proposals, the very fact he so boldly proclaims the possibilities for a revitalized America and the dream of a healed and peaceful world makes him one of the evolutionary leaders we need most right now. He reminds us that despite the darkness, light is always possible. And that itself brings forth the light.

Marianne Williamson
Los Angeles

Introduction

Have you ever felt dismayed by the state of our country and our world?

I have, and I suspect you have as well.

That dismay arises because of a deeper dream that lives in your heart and the heart of almost every American. It's a dream that goes far beyond the material fulfillment and worldly success that are the apex of the classic American Dream.

It's a recognition, on a soul level, that we are each part of something larger: a sacred plan. A destiny. A calling that goes beyond left and right politics.

We have a great and noble mission to be part of creating something magnificent with our country, something that lights up the world.

Our hearts sense that we are here to help advance that cause and create liberty and justice for all. That phrase resounds through our history because it is a call for us to remember why we are really here.

We are not here simply to create a wonderful life for ourselves and our children (although that's a fine start). We are here to demonstrate what is possible as a society and to boldly forge a brighter future with opportunity and prosperity, peace and security, health and justice.

That's why we each feel dismay and heartache with the painful evidence on the news that we're not yet accomplishing what we are here to do. When we are failing to create something extraordinary with our nation, it hurts something deep within us. We can blame our politicians, as most of us do. We can blame our system for being rigged. We can blame our fellow citizens for being deluded.

But this doesn't change the fact that each and every one of us can do something about it.

In fact, we must take responsibility for *being* the change we want to see if we are to fulfill our mission. The truth is that we didn't choose to be born in this amazing country to entertain ourselves until we die. We came here to create something special.

Fulfilling the deeper mission of America will require a contribution from all of us. Even if we've sat on the sidelines of elections. Even if we've never gotten politically involved. Even if we feel hopeless to create change. None of those stances are worthy of the nobility in our souls. We are made of finer stuff.

This book is a manifesto to help you wake up, stand in your sacred power, and take wise and effective action in the service of us fulfilling our collective mission, while expressing your own personal mission along the way. It's a book about politics that is also deeply spiritual because that is the only way our politics are going to become something we can be proud of.

It is designed to help us align our country with a higher plan, to expand our vision for what is possible, to forge innovative solutions, and to embody our sacred values for real. It's about becoming evolutionaries who build the America of tomorrow rather than impatient revolutionaries who shout ideological slogans rehearsing the past.

To do this, we will have to go beyond partisan warfare to embrace those with other political views as our deepest allies. They are also part of the team that is here to help America shine. Yes, even the people you can't stand.

In short, we need to open to a vision of possibility for our country, one in which we successfully navigate the crises, polarizations, and political warfare of today to create a country that reflects our highest ideals and that truly serves the birth of a new, global era for humanity, one that is peaceful, sustainable, healthy, and prosperous.

If you choose to take this journey with me, you will be challenged to let go of your judgments and biases—the many ways that you protect yourself and close your heart.

You'll be invited to embrace the full spectrum of American political values and integrate the virtues that each political orientation represents. You'll be called to stand passionately for your views while opening to embrace what you might have seen as the "opposition."

You'll also be invited to face America's shadow in the service of a deeper kind of patriotism that challenges us to rise to our potential. We'll look squarely at the face of genocide, slavery, and discrimination so that we can emerge more whole and committed to an America that is built on oneness, respect, and love.

After we've illuminated the path to reunite our American family, we'll explore real solutions in contentious areas, from strengthening our families to evolving our schools to stopping global warming to stabilizing the Middle East to reforming our banking. I'll show how we can forge great, bipartisan solutions more effectively than ever before.

You'll also be invited to think seriously and strategically about our long-term future and how we can create real breakthroughs with media, grassroots organizing, new forms of transpartisan political engagement, and, ultimately, forms of governance that put an end to our planet's long era of war.

As we undertake this journey, I want you to feel seen and respected for who you are and the beliefs you bring to the table, whether you are a Democrat, Republican, Independent, Libertarian, or Socialist. I will also invite you to stretch outside your comfort zone to become a more mature, thoughtful, and collaborative citizen.

Ultimately, this book is about building a movement of awake, conscious, and caring citizens who are powerfully committed to building a new era for America.

If you are willing to overturn some of your assumptions, open to a more unitive view, and roll up your sleeves to get to work, *Sacred America, Sacred World* will guide you, challenge you, and empower you to fulfill your highest role.

In this introduction, I am speaking to you directly because you have many things competing for your attention and time. I am asking you to let go of your other activities for a time and undertake a journey with me into the heart of our democracy and the heights of our shared mission.

My promise to you is that if you invest your time in reading this book, it will help you to play your unique role as a citizen of this great nation and a soul who is here to birth a better world. It will help you transform bitter partisanship and reunite our American family.

This book is thus an investment that I believe will pay dividends for you, your loved ones, and the future of our country.

Before we go further, I want to spend a bit of time sharing with you my personal journey, which began in political slumbers, passed through a phase of disillusionment, entered into the partisan fray, and ultimately arrived at a deeper level of understanding. My journey is a microcosm of the larger story of our country as we seek a higher possibility. In sharing my story, I invite you to reflect on the forces, values, and beliefs that have shaped yours. In this way, we can each begin to understand and then let go of our old identities and meet in a shared common ground as fellow Americans.

❄ ❄ ❄

Growing up in Duluth, Minnesota, with my parents Bill and Connie and my brother Mike, I felt comfortably distant from

American politics. Duluth is far from Washington, DC, literally and psychologically, as well as one of the chilliest places in the lower forty-eight states, averaging just eight degrees above zero for all of January. Nonetheless, it has a warm and welcoming community, well stocked with Scandinavians and other hardy peoples of the north. Neighbors were always eager to help, whether with chicken soup if you were sick or a snowplow if you were snowed in. We were blessed by endless acres of forests and the vast, shimmering beauty of Lake Superior, which made us all feel prosperous in natural wealth. We enjoyed a life of middle-class comfort, with top-rated public schools, more parks than we could visit, and plentiful programs for swimming, baseball, soccer, and more. People had aspirations and ambitions, but it was mostly for a settled and comfortable middle-class life.

My parents were actively involved in the community through their jobs—my father as Duluth's city attorney and my mom as a counselor for high school students and displaced homemakers—and through our Episcopal church, which reached out to the poor and marginalized. There were certainly many people in Duluth who were stuck in abusive marriages, alcoholic, or living in abject poverty. But the numbers of such people seemed small in comparison to the large and relatively content middle class. On the whole, Duluth was a modestly prosperous and healthy community—a positive example of American culture.

Local politics would periodically intrude when my father worried over his job. As the city attorney, he was a pawn in the chess match between the city council and the mayor. And because he was appointed by the mayor, he could be fired at any time. My father managed to survive decades at his post—a testament to his balanced temperament—but the crossfire exacted a toll, leaving a vague feeling in our family that politics was a life-negating force. That was the extent of my involvement with politics while growing up, aside from reading about national politics, which felt very far away.

I carried this arms-length relationship with politics into my undergraduate years at Stanford University, where I was more interested in neurobiology and psychology than politics. I read enough to be informed, though, and gradually questioned more seriously the integrity with which our country was run. But I did not truly engage the process of political change. Real change, in my view at that time, came from growth in human consciousness.

And so I devoted myself to the latest frontiers of psychology, philosophy, science, and healing. I devoured the work of pioneers of human psychology like Carl Jung, Stanislav Grof, and A. H. Almaas and integral philosophers like Sri Aurobindo, Michael Murphy, and Ken Wilber. I opened to a mystical understanding of Christianity and Sufism. I studied Hinduism and kabbalah, bodywork and aikido, meditation and shamanism—anything that promised to deliver greater wisdom. I did many ten-day silent meditation retreats and entered into a training for Holotropic Breathwork, which opened new vistas beyond the everyday mind.

During this time, Washington, DC, felt like gazing backward; it lacked the dynamism and power of the worlds I was discovering. So I largely stayed disengaged.

My real political awakening happened in 2003, when I finally allowed myself to feel heartrending dismay with the state of our country, which had grown militaristic, reactive, and fearful. The events of 9/11 could have opened the floodgates of America's heart; instead we gave in to the tyranny of revenge and war. After years of being disengaged, I finally woke up to my duty to get involved. I began to understand on a visceral level that our leaders were *my* representatives and *my* emissaries to the rest of the world.

Recognizing that my cool distance had been a form of silent support, I saw that I had to take more personal responsibility for America's policies and call forth something better from our people. Indeed, I began to see that my passion for positive change in psychology, health, spirituality, business, and other realms could not find its full and final expression until our political system passed laws and policies that supported a peaceful, sustainable, healthy, and prosperous world.

After beginning to write articles, volunteer for political campaigns, and speak truth about our political system, I kept returning to the evolutionary ideals and liberating spiritual practices I had ardently cultivated during the previous decade. I intuitively knew that they held a vital key for our political process to reflect our highest aspirations. Mahatma Gandhi had built his Indian liberation movement on disciplined spiritual practices that became *satyagraha*, a Hindu term Gandhi coined that literally means "truth force." With a foundation of equanimity and inner strength, *satyagrahis* were able to apply nonviolence in powerful ways that eventually called both the British and Indians to higher ground. Martin Luther King Jr. carried the same torch of nonviolent, spiritually based engagement that lifts people on both sides of a divide, producing profound evolution while addressing injustice.

As I sought a marriage, within my own being, of spiritual understanding and political passion, something beautiful began to emerge for the first time: a patriotic love for our country that felt intimately connected to our collective higher purpose. It took the form of a faint but growing recognition that the greatness of America's soul has yet to find its full expression, either politically or spiritually. While many celebrate our past accomplishments as the mark of America's "exceptionalism," our true greatness lies in a deeper kind of service to the world that lies in our future. I began to see that our higher mission is about America demonstrating real leadership in helping to create a world that works for all.

As I came to these realizations, my certainty grew that our "soul's code" as a country is built on timeless ideals and a spirit of service that can eventually lead us to fulfill its promise. The America I truly love is one in which the greed, self-interest, and corruption have been washed away to reveal a radiant gift for the world:

a society designed as an enlightened template to empower the best in humanity.

Our founders embedded universal ideals into the vision for our country, ideals that, while they have never been perfectly enacted, did put us on the path to throw off the shackles of old social orders and eventually create liberty and justice for all, which is still a mighty and worthy goal.

In 2003, Dennis Kucinich was the first national political leader I found who carried an aspirational vision for our country that was also grounded in deep spiritual principles. He was just beginning his presidential campaign, and in him I found a kindred spirit. While his campaign never became competitive, it provided an opportunity to turn my growing passion into action, beginning with hosting a large fundraiser for him in San Rafael, California, that featured authors Ram Dass, Shakti Gawain, and Jack Kornfield, as well as music, poetry, and mobilizing. Almost two hundred people gathered that night for passionate political talks, singing, and funky dancing. It was a new kind of political happening, and it was electric!

A frenzy of activity followed this exhilarating first night, as I created a kind of Chautauqua tour of new-paradigm political events. I organized a speaker's bureau of pioneers, authors, and musicians to bring some on the road to places like Chico, Davis, Grass Valley, and Sonoma. In our grassroots tour of "Convergences" we would find wise souls in each town who were awakening from anti-political slumber to bring a higher possibility into our political discourse.

It was an initiation into the practicalities of campaigning and an eye-opening exposure to the deeper hunger in America's citizens to have a political process that elevates us and speaks to our highest vision rather than forcing us to focus just on beating an opponent. In the course of this journey, I was hooked on forging a new kind of politics. The most satisfying aspect was finding others who had similarly yearned to have their whole being—body, mind, and soul—fully welcomed into politics.

During that period of full-throttle engagement, several people encouraged me to run for office myself someday, which I had never previously considered. I took a serious look at the matter and eventually decided that seeking elected office would not be the best channel for my skills. My talents lie more in the direction of visionary strategy. By forging new organizations, media, and writings, I can help sculpt a vision of where we are going and offer a practical roadmap of strategies to get there. I can plant seeds of change wherever the soil is ready and influence political leaders on both sides of the aisle as well as everyday citizens.

Over the years, my political orientation has evolved still further. I've supported candidates in races for Congress, the Senate, and the presidency, but I've also shifted my focus to influencing our current elected officials rather than mainly backing candidates who share my views. I've learned, through working with groups such as the Friends Committee on National Legislation, that one of the most important responsibilities of citizenship is to support, influence, and empower our elected officials to make the best choices they can, day in and day out, rather than focus solely on the next round of elections.

My political work has also evolved beyond championing progressive candidates and policies to encouraging evolution of our political culture, both left and right. While my politics still lean strongly progressive, as I've matured, I increasingly see that fulfilling our country's mission will require the best skills, insights, and policies from across the political spectrum, including conservatives, Libertarians, and moderates. Learning to respect and honor the full political spectrum leads to a stronger end result than competing with a political "enemy."

That recognition informs this entire book, which harvests the best of what I've learned in my journey of integrating spirit and politics, left and right positions, visionary future possibilities and the pragmatism of what it takes to create change. And from that vantage I now consider myself a transpartisan progressive, a term we'll explore later but that speaks to finding a higher ground in which all are honored for their views.

I have also learned that we need to transcend charismatic figures. Millions of us grew enamored with Barack Obama and the message of hope he carried powerfully in the campaign of 2008. On his victory night, I shed tears of joy that America had evolved to the level of electing a man of mixed race and stirring vision to the presidency, beginning to heal a racial schism that has long festered in our hearts. We attended the 2009 inauguration with millions of others and stood shivering on the National Mall, delighted to be part of this historic moment, waving our flags with patriotic pride.

But then, during his presidency, my elation became tempered with times of disillusionment: frustration with his appointments and policies, the fading notion of grassroots change, and partisan stalemates. In many ways, these disillusionments were necessary to dissipate the expectations many of us had for a political messiah figure. It's easier now to see the limitations of putting too much hope and expectation on anyone, including the president of the United States. It is actually a form of our political immaturity to expect someone to save and protect us rather than to stand in our own power and patiently help our system and people to evolve. Our political maturation means removing excess hope *and* excess resentment from our political figures, while offering our personal best in service to the collective challenges we face.

This holds true even if the elected leader does not share our political party. If history is our guide, we will spend about half of our lives under political leadership that does not come from our favored party. We can either spend those years resentful, frustrated, and scheming to take our power back—as much of America now does—or we can see these times as opportunities to work with people of different temperaments and values toward a shared goal of America becoming a shining light unto the world.

I now firmly believe that a single political party or ideology cannot deliver the kind of healthy, integrated, evolutionary growth that will lead America to fulfill its mission. Cultural evolution is a slow and often meandering process with many opportunities to regress. Both Democratic and Republican political positions hold value; indeed, as I've passed through the challenges of starting and successfully growing my own company, I have deepened my appreciation of free enterprise and how important it is not to restrain America's entrepreneurial engines. I've seen how the discipline, caution, and personal responsibility championed by Republicans build character and a stronger business. I have joked that I've had to integrate my "inner Republican" to become a better CEO, recognizing that some of what I once judged holds value for creating a healthy, profitable, and responsible business.

On a larger scale, I've grown to see how the evolution of our country to the next level of our potential requires the best of all of us—Republicans and Democrats, Libertarians and Greens. Our task is thus not just about getting the "right" party elected or even finding the "right" leader but about evolving our political process itself so that it generates greater wisdom and reflects the best in us. We need real, long-term solutions, and they are found in all value systems and in all parties. As we learn to appreciate alternative positions, we can help grow a healthier political culture where opponents become allies and adversaries become friends.

So the book you are holding represents the fruits of my political journey, one that started off as more radically left wing and has evolved to appreciate and even integrate positions that I once judged as of the old guard. While I still believe in progressive ideals and the vision of the future they hold, I now see that to evolve America still further, conservative and traditional values are often required to keep things working well. There's a positive evolutionary tension that progressive and conservative values create so that our movement forward is more measured, thoughtful, and grounded.

This complementarity is important to recognize and honor because it's clear that our country and our world are going through a historic shift in what we can think of as the "operating system" that runs our lives. Just as our computers are periodically upgraded with new and more sophisticated operating systems, so too are we evolving a new global consciousness and culture that will, in turn, transform every realm of human endeavor. We are evolving into one people on planet earth, and the walls between us are slowly but surely coming down in spite of the violence, tragedy, and discrimination that are still quite evident. And America must reflect that evolution as well by upgrading our own cultural codes in a balanced way.

We are only in the beginning phases of this shift and there are many ways for us to go astray, from being dragged into a World War III to becoming more isolationist to failing to meet the challenge of global warming. However, I believe that the love, courage, and stories of commitment I witness every day can carry us forward and ultimately triumph over the forces of regression, polarization, and fear.

The evolution to a truly sacred America is not an idealistic, ungrounded dream. It's an evolutionary imperative, forced by dozens of converging streams of crisis in the world, ranging from melting ice caps to emptying aquifers, from loose nukes to refugee crises, from drug wars to rogue terrorist states. The previous version of America has, in many ways, reached the limit of our capacity to produce lasting solutions to collective challenges. The world needs something more from us now, and we need something more noble from ourselves as well.

I will explore the next steps for us to become the kind of engaged, conscious, and committed citizens who can help America fulfill our country's mission and uplevel our democracy. Stepping into that next level of citizenship will also take some real reflection on where we are part of the problem. As a white American, I often want to recoil from the legacy of racial hatred that has roiled streets from Ferguson to Baltimore. To complete this book with integrity, I needed to study African American pioneers and take racial injustice seriously. To walk the talk of transpartisanship, I worked to release my judgments of conservatives by doing things I previously would have found distasteful, such as reading both of Sarah Palin's books during the 2008 election cycle and writing a public *Huffington Post* column about what I learned. I've made microloans to Islamic entrepreneurs, engaged in healing work with Indigenous peoples, and slept in an Occupy encampment. Writing this book over the last ten years has thus compelled me to expand the compass of my own heart as I call to my fellow Americans to do the same.

So that summarizes my journey that has led to the book that you hold in your hands. While I will weave some parts of my personal story and experiences into the rest of the book, *Sacred America, Sacred World* is ultimately a vision and strategic roadmap for the evolution of our country, offered with as much clarity and simplicity as I can muster. My intent is to honor the importance of each of us in forging our nation's future, whether we identify as progressive or conservative, atheistic or religious, Indigenous or European, white or black, male or female, working class or wealthy. I aim to infuse that inclusive spirit in each sentence of this book.

In the pages that follow, I will explore four main areas that will be essential for America to fulfill our higher mission. In Part One, Developing a Sacred Worldview, we will look at the emergence of a more holistic and reverential way of seeing the world, one that is coded into our founding ideals as well as emergent as we enter a global era. I liken this to a new operating system and show how we are upgrading both our consciousness and our culture. In Part Two, I'll address how we can become more whole as a people by healing the divides in our society, which are ultimately rooted in our consciousness. I end by recognizing that this is vital to "Occupy the 100 Percent" and enter into a new era without leaving anyone behind. In Part Three, Creating Innovative Solutions, I'll look at how a sacred and transpartisan perspective can lead to powerful and effective policies that lead to stronger families, improved schools, peaceful communities, and a healthier economy, in addition to a sustainable world. I will share many exciting examples and break-throughs here. In Part Four, Building an Evolutionary Movement, I'll look at how to build an effective political movement for long-term change, going beyond left and right to address the deepest needs for evolving our country and world. I will share about exciting work under way to create unified campaigns and an infrastructure for the empowerment of conscious citizens. And I will culminate with an exploration of how we can evolve global democracy in a way that finally creates a world at peace.

While I cover a lot of ground, a book like this cannot be com-prehensive or complete. My hope is that *Sacred America, Sacred World* will help awaken *your* dreams for our country and inspire you to take passionate action, for it is in the synergy of working together that something truly historic can be born.

PART ONE

Developing a Sacred Worldview

Part One of this book is devoted to the deepest level of change in our country's worldview, which in turn drives our values, visions, and policies. The task of evolving a sacred worldview is at the core of evolving a healthier, happier, and more prosperous country that serves as a beacon of light for the world.

Psychologists have shown that individuals pass through many stages in their moral, emotional, and intellectual growth from birth to adulthood. Our country is no different because it largely reflects the growth in our citizens as a whole. Through our daily choices, words, actions, and votes, we sculpt a world in alignment with our vision and values. Thus, as our consciousness lifts, so does our country.

In this part, I explore the sacred worldview that I see emerging for our country. A sacred worldview is one in which all are honored and treated with dignity, regardless of ideology, party, philosophy, race, or identity. It is a global worldview that sees us as one human family.

Sociological evidence from researchers such as Dr. Paul H. Ray describes the emergence of a new value system in the last fifty years that has led to the formation of the Cultural Creatives.

These values reflect that America is beginning to evolve beyond the worldview that has been predominant for many decades—the rational-individualistic-materialistic paradigm. We are evolving a more integrated view of systems, a more inclusive philosophy, and a more compassionate global understanding. These emerging values ultimately support a sacred worldview in which we all find common ground. A sacred worldview is built on reverence and respect for all.

The emergence of a worldview based on reverence for all is thus the bigger theme of this part of the book, which lays the groundwork for the rest of the societal changes I believe are required for the next evolution of our country.

America 7.0

If we are to have peace on earth, our loyalties must become ecumenical rather than sectional. Our loyalties must transcend our race, our tribe, our class, and our nation; and this means we must develop a world perspective.
—Martin Luther King Jr.

WHEN OUR FOUNDING FATHERS risked their lives to sign the Declaration of Independence, America became a free country. It was a truly historic moment. From that point forward, we Americans have had to rely on ourselves to govern, regulate our economy, pass laws, and organize a common defense, as well as protect the rights and liberties of our citizens. In other words, we had to build a new "operating system" for our country, which we can think of as the foundational assumptions, laws, and social institutions that allow us to operate together.

The first attempt to organize our activities involved the Articles of Confederation—a way for states that were at the time highly suspicious of any centralized power to form a loose national confederation while retaining most of their power. In the language of software operating systems, we can view this as America 1.0. Looking in the rearview mirror of history, the Articles of Confederation seems to be an exciting triumph. In practice, it proved to be a mess.

Interstate traders had different currencies to deal with, as well as tariffs that drove down the profitability of trade. There was no way to raise money for a national army, which left the newly formed United States of America poorly defended. And there was neither a national executive to make decisions nor courts to which states could appeal disputes.

The poor performance of our 1.0 operating system led early American leaders to almost immediately begin thinking about an upgrade. The Constitutional Convention faced all the problems and inefficiencies created by the Articles of Confederation and devised our Constitution, which was ratified in 1787 to create the current federal system, which balanced power better between the federal government and the states and laid out the balance of powers between different branches of government in a clear way. This upgrade to a 2.0 operating system for our country was an enormous advance not only for America but for the world, which received a new template for democracy.

Our Constitution continues to shape every aspect of our current American society. However, it was designed such that new laws, protections, beliefs, and values can evolve on top of this core, a process that has distinct parallels with building new operating systems on top of the original base of code. In many ways, each upgrade of the operating system represents a deeper application of the sacred principles built into America from the beginning, which we'll be exploring more throughout the book.

Historians differ in what they see as the major fulcrum points in the history of America, often choosing to focus on wars or presidential administrations. I see America's growth through the lens of the evolution of new levels of consciousness that expand our respect for the freedoms and rights of others and which are then institutionalized in the form of law. This view of our history does not dwell on lateral expansions, such as the addition of states, or on external wars, which reflect how we engage with other countries.

Instead, I see the deepest and most enduring activities as those that lead to an evolution in our worldview and the societal systems that support it. To help understand these, again, I use the metaphor of the evolution of computer operating systems. Here is my list of the major upgrades to the American operating system in the last 240 years:

1. *America 1.0 (1776–1787)*: Nation is born; Articles of Confederation

2. *America 2.0 (1787–1865)*: Constitution and Bill of Rights

3. *America 3.0 (1865–1920)*: Slavery is abolished

4. *America 4.0 (1920–1933)*: Women included as voting citizens

5. *America 5.0 (1933–1960)*: New Deal legislation expands role of government to create safety nets

6. *America 6.0 (1960–2000)*: Civil rights movement and women's movement expand full inclusion of more citizens

7. *America 7.0 (2000–present)*: Emergence of truly global era, with globalized Internet, trade, travel, and movement of finance

In most of the upgrades, a precipitating crisis reveals design flaws in the beliefs, values, principles, or practices built into the last operating system. After passing through the crisis, which typically sheds light on the problems of the last operating system, there is an expansion of freedoms and rights along with better safeguards to institutionalize the advances of the past and to protect those who have been disenfranchised. For example:

- *Problem*: South secedes from the Union → 3.0 upgrade without slavery

- *Problem*: Great Depression → 5.0 upgrade with a better societal safety net and financial protections

- *Problem*: Social unrest of the sixties → 6.0 upgrade with more integrated society and protected civil rights

Before each new evolution, we often pass through a period of increased resistance to change. This time of stability is an essential part of integrating the gains of the past and allowing them to become part of the new "tradition" of our society. However, the stabilizing aspect of tradition can turn into stagnancy and block further evolution. So something needs to stoke the fires of change. In addition to the collective crises that give a "push," inspiring leaders emerge that offer a "pull" to lead American society forward, visionaries such as John Adams, Thomas Jefferson, Abraham Lincoln, Susan B. Anthony, Franklin D. Roosevelt, and Martin Luther King Jr.

The upgrade to America 7.0 hasn't been distinguished by a singular crisis as an evolutionary driver but a series of them that have begun to force a shift in our orientation from being nation-centered to being global citizens. Financially, the market crash of 2000 followed by the much more major 2008–2009 global meltdown began to reveal how deeply interconnected we all are economically. In the first fifteen years of the new millennium, we've been roiled by the spread of terrorism, fear of global pandemics like Ebola, and an increasing challenge to the sustainability of our planetary ecosystems. All of these crises are forcing us to begin to think and act out of concern for the whole world rather than just America. That's because we are globally interconnected now to a degree that is unprecedented in history, which has been driven by the rapid interconnection of the Internet as well as finance, trade, media, and travel.

The America 7.0 operating system is thus slowly emerging in the first decades of this century, pushed by many evolutionary drivers. It's leading us toward a fundamentally new operating system for our country that will take decades to fully realize even while some changes have already begun to emerge. It is our first truly global operating system, which corresponds with a real sense of becoming global citizens. At the root level, America's 7.0 operating system is built upon the evolution of a new level of consciousness as a country, which then leads to a new set of governing assumptions, political structures, and our national psychology. The operating system of our nation cannot simply reject the old code. It must evolve in an integrated fashion, which means completing the unfinished parts of the last stage. That's why our maturation as a country requires facing what is no longer helpful about our beliefs, thoughts, and habits as well as what we've hidden in our shadows, which we will explore more later in the book.

For example, the presidency of George W. Bush caused angst for many people committed to the new global operating system, partially because his "go it alone" style of foreign policy felt increasingly out of sync. In this way, President Bush provided an exaggeration of some of the independent and nationalistic assumptions that we are outgrowing, which was actually helpful in the long range, provoking a clarification of where we are going, which is increasingly toward interdependence and collaboration.

However, to move forward, we need to also embrace what was virtuous and valuable about Bush and his allies rather than only pointing at problems and inadequacies. After all, they represent aspects of the American character that we need to build upon in America 7.0. Growth rarely happens through self-hatred, even while it does require rigorous self-reflection. Shifting the core patterns requires releasing our judgments and finding appreciation for the perceived "problems" of the past. That spirit of love and acceptance is a foundation for the deeper changes to happen. For America 7.0 to be a true upgrade, we cannot jettison the old but need to build upon and extend it. If not, we compromise the efficacy of the new platform.

In America's next operating system, we need the strong, single-pointed, and resolute warrior who is willing to stand for what he believes is right, something obvious in President Bush's administration. Simply rejecting the warrior values outright will not work. That would be like deleting essential lines of code from the next operating system. What we need is to upgrade the warrior and integrate him with the emerging global operating system. It's not the warrior qualities in Bush that were the problem; it's the use of those qualities in situations for which they did not represent skillful means.

Integration is the main difference between an upgrade and a rebellion. The values of a rebellion tend to be in opposition to the dominant culture's values. They are countercultural rather than transcultural. When in rebellion, we enter a tug-of-war for dominance; it's either the old operating system or its antithesis. A true upgrade, though, transcends and includes both polarities while letting go of what no longer serves. When that happens, the warring factions recognize that their most important priorities have been honored in a new viewpoint that is more whole.

All of this relates to the importance of exploring our country's shadow. Doing so with rigor is a requirement to activate a new system because it allows us to see the inadequacies of the last stage more clearly. We need to recognize where we have been unconscious, blind, or untruthful with ourselves so as to help less-developed parts of our national character to find their next-higher expression.

The 7.0 operating system for America is very much a global operating system. It is not defined by thinking only of American citizens but by expanding our care for the world. It requires releasing old animosities and building new strategic alliances. It builds upon a global Internet and media, with international travel growing each year. Most of all, America 7.0 is about seeing ourselves as global citizens *and* American citizens, as an increasing number of us do.[1]

As we have now entered the transition to America 7.0, the culture of America 6.0, which is more rooted in identities of religion, race, and nation, is still prominent but starting to decline. These two cultures are not defined by skin color, language, ethnic group, or religion. They represent ways of seeing the world that have unique national expressions while transcending the borders between nation-states.

The declining culture is one in which the boundaries of community, identity, and concern are focused on the national level or still more partial identities of race, class, religion, or party. For those on the inside of our boundary of "us," we champion the best for them. Within this in-group, we mostly align our economic interests. For those on the outside of this boundary, we retain a certain suspicion, a protective looking out for "our" interests versus theirs. In the more extreme forms, it can result in xenophobia and extreme nationalism that is based in discrimination, as we see in some extreme right parties.

This strong sense of national identity is reflected in the distribution of military forces—no forces are focused on protecting boundaries between American states, for example, while massive resources are allocated to potential disputes with other countries. When most US citizens are asked who they are, they are likely to say "American" before saying, "I'm a Minnesotan" or "I'm a global citizen." When we watch the Olympics, the coverage focuses on "our" team. The medal count becomes a measure of our national worth in competition with other nations. Similarly, when reporting on armed conflicts or natural disasters, the primary concern is how many of "our" people were injured or killed. The total body count, if even reported, is largely secondary.

Although it remains dominant, this nation-centered culture is declining in power. On the Internet, national boundaries are nonexistent. In commerce, we are increasingly an interconnected world, with transnational corporations operating globally. Our environmental challenges do not respect national boundaries. Science is a global endeavor, as is finance. Even our entertainment, food, and travel are all increasingly global.

So, while nation-centered culture still wields great political power, the underpinning psychology and infrastructure are starting to shift in dramatic ways, which will ultimately mean a shift toward a global sense of culture and identity. Eventually, we'll be more concerned with how many people died in an earthquake than how many Americans. We'll be more likely to celebrate the best athlete's achievements than the best American's. We'll champion global accords when addressing environmental challenges rather than focusing on narrowly defined national interests. The ascending culture of America 7.0 is thus global in its sense of identity and sphere of concern. It is grounded in a unified sense of community with the whole planet rather than separating people into enemies and friends.

As the interweaving of nations and the evolution of global consciousness proceed further and we evolve more reliable structures for global peacemaking, it will eventually make large militaries less necessary, gradually replaced by smaller police forces to protect the peace within nations. En route to that endpoint, though, we face many challenges, the primary one for America being the balance between the security that our current military power can provide and the decrease in our nationalistic focus that is required for the long-term health of ourselves and our world.

That's why the task of honoring (and seeing clearly) what has gone before us is so important. If the transition to the ascending global operating system is too abrupt, we may undermine the foundations for its emergence by rejecting the economic and military stabilizing force that we now offer. We would risk leaving behind the values of the conservative right that support family, local community, and national sovereignty.

The ascending culture needs time to mature and grow structures of support and collaboration. Millions of people need to evolve their worldview. Organizationally, the ascending culture needs media, institutions, and political platforms that embody and reinforce its global focus.

America is thus in a pivotal position to help usher in a new era. To the extent that we cling to our 6.0 alpha-dominant–nationalistic status for too long, we become the problem that the rest of the world needs to address. If we shift our alpha-dominant status too early, destructive ethnic, religious, and tribal rivalries will flare up at the same time that we face mounting global crises that require a coherent response. That's why we are best served to honor what has made our country successful while fostering new initiatives that are global in their scope, while we test out what works.

For America to play a leadership role in the next stage of our planet's evolution, as I believe was imprinted in the founding codes of our country, we must see ourselves as champions of the ascending 7.0 global culture while also respecting the 6.0 America-centric culture and its gifts. As the ascending culture gains prominence in the coming decades, there will be a relaxation of the tension that characterizes the boundaries between countries. From a spiritual perspective, these boundaries create an uncomfortable friction that can eventually erupt as war and conflict. This friction wastes money, time, and resources. Evolving a truly global perspective will eventually eliminate the need to protect artificial borders and thus open to the possibility of a far freer and more prosperous world.

America 7.0 holds great promise, not only for our citizens but for the entire world. It is a fulfillment of millennia of cultural evolution, striving toward better systems of governance, culture, and consciousness. It may not be our last operating system, but I believe it is the operating system that can help us transition to a peaceful and thriving planet. And that will be a gift for which we will all be eternally grateful.

2

What Is a Sacred America?

A very great vision is needed, and the man who has it must follow it
as the eagle seeks the deepest blue of the sky.
—Crazy Horse

IN THIS CHAPTER, we're ready to flesh out more of what it will look like to live into the reality of a truly sacred America.

In our current era, America has developed a mixed reputation: innovative, idealistic, and bold on the one hand; wasteful, arrogant, and self-interested on the other. When we add the term "sacred" in front of "America," many people who are committed to positive change might fear a kind of righteousness that blinds us to our shadows, inflates our sense of self-worth, and rails against whatever is not "sacred."

I have just the opposite in mind. For me, sacred is a term that recognizes the dignity, divinity, and wholeness in literally everyone and everything. It binds us together in the mystery of life and links us into a single human family. In a truly sacred world, no one is ultimately our enemy. A sacred worldview recognizes that we are all children of divinity, albeit children who forget our shared parentage and squabble over inconsequential matters.

We then connect the term "sacred" to America. America means many things to the world, ranging from a shining city on the hill that flies the flag of freedom to a feared military empire. At our current stage of development, we are a complex mixture of high ideals and selfish motives, great generosity and shocking apathy. We achieve breathtaking things that few believed possible but then are often triumphant about our greatness in a way that blinds us to our shadow.

Much can be said about the current state of America's character, but perhaps the most central is that America has a pioneering spirit, always experimenting to find something that works better, never resting solely on our past, constantly seeking the newest frontier. We are not a country that stagnates for long; America is a roaring engine for evolution, which is evident in everything from our go-go startup culture to exhilarating breakthroughs in entertainment.

It is that spirit of innovation, adventure, and possibility that needs to inform this exploration of what happens when "sacred" and "America" come together. Sacred America is more than part of a book title. It's a call for us to reach for our highest destiny as a country. We are called to explore new frontiers politically, economically, and even spiritually, not just in service to our own citizens, but in service to the world. Our experiment in building a free and democratic society can help to break the shackles of others who remain fettered. The story of America aims us toward a truly noble future, one in which we help finally put to rest the horrors of the past millennia, from slavery to hunger to war.

A sacred vision for America is thus one in which America is helping to advance the next stage of planetary evolution out of a sense of compassion, service, and dedication while modeling the changes that are needed first within our own borders. As the most influential superpower, America's leadership will be essential to successfully address our collective challenges. We can choose to be a champion of breakthroughs, leading the way to new global solutions. Or we can resist, focus only on our interests, and become seen as a self-centered empire builder, which may precipitate our decline, like self-enamored empires of the past.

If we choose wisely, we can help midwife a new kind of peaceful and prosperous planetary culture unparalleled in history. To do so, though, many shifts will be required in how we see ourselves and our role in the world. We'll need new approaches to public problem solving and reformed structures of government, better systems of education and deeper forms of community, innovative approaches to diplomacy and integrative models of healing, sustainable businesses and lower-impact lifestyles. The list of shifts is vast, but I believe they can be synthesized into a new dream of what America can still become, along with specific strategies to make such a dream real.

A new and improved American Dream can put in motion deep shifts not only in our social and political systems, but also in the growth of our citizens. Without a more educated, enlightened, creative, and healthy citizenry, political and economic reforms will flounder. Reforms that fail to address the maturation of our citizens will likely fail. That's why the evolution of America cannot be separated from the evolution of our citizens, which in turn requires a vision that inspires us to grow still further.

And so we start the next phase of our journey into a truly sacred America (and ultimately, a sacred world) with a vision, which is like a homing device we place in our future that magnetically draws us forward. When we envision the future with vivid detail, we begin to activate that vision in others and attract the resources necessary to bring it into being. The suffragettes envisioned a future in which women were the political equals of men, despite all the historical evidence to the contrary. Those who abolished slavery knew that a freer future for African Americans was possible, again despite hundreds of years of the opposite. Those visions helped them weather the setbacks of the day and move our country forward.

Standing in today's America and looking forward into a 7.0 future, I vividly see us contributing to the creation of a world that has evolved beyond war. Some day, children will read in their history books of millions dying in vast battles over territory. They will open their eyes wide, asking their parents, "Did people *really* used to do that to each other?" As part of creating that future, I envision America evolving from the greatest military power in the world into the greatest peacemaking power. We will lead the way in training the peace leaders of tomorrow—the facilitators, social engineers, artists, psychologists, healers, and teachers who will be on the front lines, defusing conflicts before they metastasize into wars and healing wounds before they fester.

I see a future in which America has dramatically shifted from consumer wastefulness to become a model for sustainability, powered by clean energy and efficient use of resources. I see us taking full responsibility for our contribution to climate change, for cleaning up our extraordinary land and beautiful seas, and for preserving pristine (and vital) ecosystems. I see us becoming a powerhouse of green innovations, catching up with countries like Germany to play a leadership role in the new "green collar economy"[1] that creates abundance, opportunity, and jobs while easing our impact on the planet. I see thriving communities built on these new technologies that are sustainable, livable, and whole.

In America's future, I also see us leading the way in health care, reforming hospitals to integrate holistic approaches to health and teaching effective methods of self-healing, as well as creating sophisticated education and media programs that shift our habits around lifestyle, nutrition, and exercise.

I also envision an America in which we have better balanced the vital dynamism of free markets with the wisdom of social and environmental safeguards, ensuring that the companies that deliver great products *and* improve our world are the engine that drives not just our economy, but the entire world's. I see America embracing reforms that ensure corporations are even more accountable and transparent in a way that lets markets reward the best not only in serving us products but in serving all the stakeholders in our society. And I see us putting the incentives and safeguards in place to ensure an economy that truly has opportunity for all.

In this future vision, America will have taken seriously the importance of healing our history with Indigenous people and African Americans. I see a climate of respect, dignity, and honoring, as well as fair and equal treatment within our systems of justice, which will increasingly focus on restoration rather than retribution, cutting our prison populations to a fraction of their current size.

I see this shift in our justice systems freeing resources for empowering more of our young citizens with quality education that prepares them to be responsible, creative, and contributing members of society. I see an education system that takes seriously the need for social and emotional-intelligence education as well as training in the skills to become a good marriage partner and family member.

Finally, I see America leading the way in the emergence of new, vibrant structures of democratic participation on a global scale, with governing bodies that ensure the global rule of wisdom rather than war. This will be part of a shift from a paradigm of global dominance to one of collaboration, in which America's leadership does not derive from overpowering others but from honoring all voices in creating a cohesive and peaceful global community.

That vision is achievable if we choose to make it so. Making that vision real is the foundation of this entire book.

3

The Next American Dream

All our dreams can come true—if we
have the courage to pursue them.
—Walt Disney

EVERY ERA CARRIES ITS version of the American Dream, often told through the story of a hero who triumphs over obstacles to reach the summit of success. We love our Horatio Algers who overcome poverty to find wealth. We revere our Founding Fathers who threw off the oppressive yoke of Britain. We celebrate our scientists who put a man on the moon. We need our dreams, ideals, and heroes to provide meaning for our lives.

For the current phase of American history, our American Dream has become increasingly focused on material fulfillment. The dream of home ownership, a white picket fence, and two cars in the garage has grown into one that envisions a mansion, a vacation home, and a yacht. Our impulse toward more—which is at the core of our natural evolutionary drive—has too often failed to move toward higher levels of our creative expression and fulfillment. So we end up just wanting more and more "stuff." In that way, our desire for "more" fails to transition to an American Dream that is focused on more happiness, meaning, adventure, service, and joy rather than material accumulation. This contradicts the research, which shows that materialism actually undermines well-being, while real happiness comes from quality relationships, personal growth, and a sense of meaning.[1]

Achieving a materialistic dream can certainly build good virtues—entrepreneurship and hard work, thrift and discipline. It can train us in some aspects of living a sacred life. Indeed, building a safe, comfortable, and beautiful nest for our family is a noble endeavor. However, what happens when we fail to uplevel our dream is that we keep expanding the American Dream laterally, filling our homes with ever more things. We "fatten" the dream rather than deepen it. We accumulate excess in our garages, closets, attics, and around our midriffs. And we build ever-larger castles to accommodate our ever-expanding roster of possessions.

At the same time, we've colluded in creating an economy in which more and more of our citizens can no longer participate in any kind of American Dream, which leads us to wall off from their misery while they envy us. The stark contrast of material inequality sows the seeds for much social unrest as the perception of unfairness is toxic to the well-being of a society.

As we increase the bloat at the upper levels, our American Dream becomes stagnant, leading to a life of material excess that does not foster a sustainable society (or real happiness). We become consumers rather than creators, viewers rather than citizens. We sit on oversized sofas watching enormous TVs in houses that far outstrip our actual needs. And then we spend much of our life energy on earning the money to support this level of material overabundance.

The current version of the American Dream, while once a noble focus for our aspirations, has largely failed to mature into its next level of sacred expression. A solely consumerist, materialist dream does not elicit our full potential nor inspire a life of meaning and can often distract from the quality relationships that are more central to happiness.

Our American Dream is a guiding light that motivates us, moves us forward, and shapes our daily activities. When we have a dream that is unworthy of us, we forget who we are. A truly sacred America needs a new dream for our citizens, a dream that calls upon our full, creative potential to make a contribution to the world. Instead of "having it all," our dream might evolve to living a life that is a "blessing for all" or "in service to all."

By living in alignment with a new and higher dream, we free up more of our life energy for the cultivation of greater virtue and skill in accomplishing that dream. Instead of spending our time buying and repairing things, we can spend our life force on becoming a new Renaissance man or woman—creative, conscious, successful, generous, adventurous, balanced, and loving. We can do more and have less—with more freedom!

The way I see it, an upgraded American Dream will need to unify two of our oldest dreams into a higher-level hybrid—the dream of worldly success and the dream of spiritual realization. Traditionally, to achieve spiritual realization meant renouncing worldly life for the desert, monastery, or ashram to allow a life of uninterrupted contemplation or prayer. The price tag for a life of spiritual riches was a life of material poverty. And vice versa, the demands of a life of family, career, and worldly responsibilities often left little time for meditation, prayer, or devotion to spiritual life. What this effectively did was to create lopsided people. Those in worldly power had an atrophied inner life and often lacked real wisdom, joy, and fulfillment. Those in spiritual or religious enclaves were joyful and awake but had an atrophied outer life. Each side became adept at its half of the developmental equation but did not truly understand the other.

The emergence of a new American Dream comes from the merger of these two currents into one beautiful river—the river of living as what author Andrew Harvey calls a "divine human." A divine human is a literal expression of the soul. A divine human lives in radiant alignment with the highest level of consciousness, but is fully and passionately engaged in the world. It is different from Eastern models of enlightenment in the past, which often focused on transcending worldly life; instead, a divine human lives as a unique expression of his or her essence *within* the world. It is a model of spiritual realization that fundamentally embraces service and expresses a new kind of unity. It is enlightenment in action.

It also goes beyond solely focusing on our own liberation to recognize our deep interconnection with others and the need to act out of concern for that larger whole. Becoming a divine human means shifting from a focus on "me" to "we." The African word *ubuntu* is an expression of this shift and means "I am because you are." It points us in the direction of spiritual practice as a community, as the best of our churches, synagogues, and mosques encourage, which leads to a natural flow of generosity and support to others.

This informs our exploration of a new American Dream, which integrates two streams—the spiritual realization of the mystic with the life mastery of the person of the world. The heroes and heroines of our next American era are those who have achieved real impact in society through wise and strategic action, but married with inner depth. They take the time to open to their most authentic selves and then express that in worldly leadership of companies, nonprofits, and governments. They live lives that are inwardly and outwardly fulfilled, rich in creativity while also having family, friends, and organizations that support their gifts. They go beyond having a career to having a meaningful calling. As they align their lives with that calling and simultaneously take the time for healing, spiritual practice, and vibrant health, their personal lives support the expression of that calling. They live a life of authenticity and purpose, radiant with the knowledge that they are vessels for grace and an expression of a larger mission.

In this next American Dream, the boundaries will dissolve between the meditator on the mountaintop and the entrepreneur in the marketplace. We need both their skills and talents to create a truly divine human life. On a material level, the next American Dream will no longer celebrate material excess to the same degree. Mansions filled with trinkets and toys will be seen as sad expressions of an atrophied inner life. A lovely home that is sustainably designed, comfortable, and beautiful, without excess, will be sufficient for the heroes and heroines of the new American Dream. Our garages will be spacious, with plenty of room for plug-in electric vehicles, powered by solar panels on the roofs. Our yards will be filled with vegetables that we grow ourselves, keeping us in deeper connection with the earth. We will satisfy the essentials of our current American Dream with less money and less time, freeing up more of our life force for living a truly creative life. And by this embrace of more simplicity, we will not only become happier but also free up resources for those who have yet to achieve the most basic levels of the American Dream.

A life that is balanced between inner growth and outer success is ultimately more fulfilling and more meaningful than one in which we are gorging ourselves materially while befouling the planet. When we are no longer so desperate in our need for possessions, accolades, or awards, we can connect with each other in more authentic ways. We can create space and time for the enjoyment of life's simple pleasures.

The next American Dream is one in which our sacredness finds expression in every aspect of our lives. It is the way I truly believe we were born to live, expressing our creative powers in reverence for this beautiful world, leaving behind our unique flourishes on the evolving canvas of human culture and a legacy of happy, healthy communities for generations to come.

That is an American Dream that is worthy of our true nature.

4

E Pluribus Unum

*We don't accomplish anything in this world alone ... and whatever
happens is the result of the whole tapestry of one's life and all the weavings
of individual threads from one to another that creates something.*
—Sandra Day O'Connor

NEXT I WANT TO explore our nation's official motto, which I
believe offers important clues and a profound compass setting for
how we can live into the next level of our destiny as a nation.

The Great Seal of the United States, which we find on today's
dollar bill, contains the Latin motto *E pluribus unum* ("Out of many,
one") in the beak of the eagle. At the time of the adoption of this
motto, *E pluribus unum* reflected the unification of thirteen states
into one nation, as depicted by the thirteen arrows in the left claw
of the eagle and the thirteen-leafed olive branch in the right claw.

This motto can be seen as a commitment embedded in the
founding codes of our country that can help us chart the path forward into the evolution of America 7.0. If the motto were only a
celebration of a new political alliance, we might assume our country's mission was completed long ago: a singular feat of rebellion,
independence, and nation founding. However, the original thirteen
colonies have grown into fifty states, covering a geographic area
more than ten times the size of the original colonies. The mission

of creating a greater union has thus been an ongoing journey rather than a singular moment.

If we take E pluribus unum seriously, it even points beyond political alliances to a spiritual role that America has charted for itself: to lead toward greater wholes. We find this higher purpose reflected in the stars above the eagle's head, which are arranged in a Star of David, an ancient symbol for the bridging of heaven and earth. The political and spiritual aspects of E pluribus unum go hand in hand; the creation of larger political unions requires a shift in identity toward that greater whole. Without such a shift, we would always think of ourselves as Californians or Minnesotans rather than Americans.

On the spiritual side, we discover that we are more virtuous, more fulfilled, and stronger through our active participation in a greater whole rather than through our isolation. When we recognize our oneness, we stop fearing, hating, or attempting to destroy the perceived other. We expand the boundaries of "our" tribe.

War is an expression of our "manyness" and sense of separation, whereas peace is an expression of our "oneness." Seen more deeply, then, America's motto charts a course for our country to lead beyond the wars that have characterized a very long epoch of human civilization—a time of perceived manyness—to an era in which our sense of oneness prevails. That is why the eagle's head on the seal is turned toward the talon holding the olive branch, a symbol of peace. The ultimate mission of America, coded in us from the founding, can be seen as the spreading of peace.

Over the last centuries, America has had growing pains in putting E pluribus unum into practice. For much of our history, our human tendency to identify with manyness has fueled racial injustice, beginning with slavery and moving into less overt forms of racism, which we still struggle to move beyond. The impulse toward racism runs counter to our motto and the sacred truth of oneness.

The same is true of the subordination of women, which reinforces the sense of manyness in opposition to a spirit of oneness.

Many reforms in the spirit of E pluribus unum are on their way to completion. Others have just begun, such as our full embrace of homosexuality, immigrants, African Americans, Native Americans, and we could even say members of other political parties. With each passing decade, our motto calls upon us to evolve still further. It calls us to illuminate where are we exaggerating divides rather than finding where our interests, ideals, and dreams coincide.

In today's political environment, the motto E pluribus unum encourages us to strengthen cross-party friendships and alliances, as well as enter into global accords, agreements, and partnerships. A narrowly defined self-interest in trade, for instance, perpetuates the sense of manyness in the world rather than our oneness. Spiritually, aligning with E pluribus unum means we need to outgrow seeing ourselves primarily as Americans and begin to foster a sense of ourselves as global citizens, which has been happening at a remarkable pace, as evidenced by a 2008 study in which 71 percent of Americans agreed with the statement, "I see myself as a citizen of Planet Earth as well as an American."[1]

When we see ourselves exclusively as Americans who are looking out only for "our" separate interests and "our" lifestyle, we perpetuate the sense of manyness that breeds war, suspicion, and mistrust. Seeing ourselves as global citizens is a powerful step toward oneness. By aligning our country politically and spiritually with our motto, America can help advance the historic transition beyond a culture of violence to an enduring culture of peace.

And that is why I believe that E pluribus unum was inscribed on our most sacred seal: it is a call for us all to remember our true purpose here and to help us evolve an ever more perfect union, not just within our current borders but with the world as a whole.

PART TWO

Evolving Our Consciousness

After we have laid the groundwork for understanding the foundations of a sacred worldview and how it applies to the evolution of America, our next task is to see the many ways that we are not yet living in a sacred way and to evolve toward greater wholeness.

This wholeness is especially important in the political arena since the images, media, and beliefs we inherit are invariably filled with polarization, misunderstandings, and disrespect. This is especially true when it comes to other political parties, races, genders, and classes. We learn to identify with one side of a polarity and lose our sense of oneness.

In this part of the book, we begin to bring alive the promise of a sacred worldview by discovering that we are more whole, balanced, and wise when we can fully experience our unity with the "other."

Ultimately, living in a sacred way is about making oneness real. That also means seeing how we complete the unresolved histories of our ancestors. We will engage in some deep shadow work in this part, facing the darker side of American history and American power, which begins the process of releasing our history of genocide, oppression, racism, and classism until we emerge more whole.

5

Radicals and Republicans

For some time now, we have all fallen into a pattern of describing our choice as left or right. It has become standard rhetoric in discussions of political philosophy. But is that really an accurate description of the choice before us? ... Isn't our choice really not one of left or right, but of up or down ...
—Ronald Reagan

AN ESSENTIAL PART OF activating a sacred vision for America is going beyond exclusive, polarized political identities, which we'll be exploring more throughout this book. This happens not by erasing our natural differences but by understanding and appreciating those differences in a wider context. Seen deeply enough, the values carried by radical left-wingers and rock-ribbed Republicans are both required for America to step into greater maturity as a country. If we can compassionately hold the full spectrum, we can devise better solutions and create a more unified culture.

Our political process, though, tends to drive people toward increasingly fixed political beliefs that are reinforced by watching media and befriending people exclusively from the same party. As our left- and right-wing political cultures become more and more separate, we also start to favor more identity-driven political leaders. Our candidates evolve into ever more perfect expressions of each party's values as they respond to the pressures of voters, the media, and their party. Social networks and clubs also then attract people of the same values and reinforce their beliefs.

Once we hold rigidly to one identity, our growth can be slowed or even arrested altogether. We stop valuing other perspectives and privilege our values over others. To navigate this critical crossroads in history, it is essential to expand our sense of identity, deeply listen to those with different opinions, and work toward collaboration and synergy. And that depends on each of us opening to the real value of political positions we may not like much at all. Seeing political identities from a higher level enhances our appreciation of the value each holds.

One way to think about the political spectrum that I have found helpful is to consider different groups as representing different kinds of relationships with our life force—the vital energy that powers our lives. This life force can express itself on many levels, from our physical activity to our sexuality to how we wear our hair and how we manage our money. It also applies to how we manage life force in the form of companies, organizations, and governments.

The more radical and experimental wing aims to let this life force express itself in novel, free-flowing ways. It often wants more freedom with less responsibility. Burning Man is a famously freewheeling example: the yearly sixty-thousand-person festival and experiment in communal living in the Nevada desert includes massive art installments, themed camps, all-night parties, and a money-free economy. During one of the two years that my wife and I attended, I was most struck by a man who memorized some two hundred poems, donned a jukebox costume, and wandered the desert whispering a randomized poem from his collection in the ear of whoever pushed the jukebox "button." It was remarkably creative, artistic, intimate, and generous—radically experimental values at their best.

The conservative camp often prizes the opposite virtue: disciplined mastery over our life force. Military training offers the pinnacle of this perspective, with its intense physical training, loyalty to regulations, sacrifice for country, and a clear chain of command. It involves protecting what we cherish, including family and personal property, as well as disciplining our life force to move according to our will and the will of our commanders. When we think of men hitting the beaches of Normandy to face nearly certain death, we cannot help but be moved by the nobility in the sacrifice, which represents conservative values at their best.

This polarity shows up in many ways. Liberals are more likely to experiment with communal living, blending personal boundaries into shared spaces. Republicans are more likely to be members of the NRA to protect their personal property with force if necessary. Liberals tend to question or dismiss tradition. Conservatives revere it. Liberals often prefer the freedom-laden term "spirituality." Conservatives tend toward religion, which literally comes from the root *ligare*, which means "to bind." Liberal men are more likely to wear long hair than conservative men, who tend to prefer short hair. Liberals want more government generosity (symbolic of a free flow of energy); conservatives generally want less.

Even insults are illustrative: "Flaming liberal" evokes an image of someone with an uncontrolled flow of life force. "Button-down conservative" describes someone holding his or her body to control the flow of energy. Neither side tends to respect the other, but in the larger view these two approaches are important complements to each other in the design and evolution of a society. Too much liberal experimentation and the secure foundations of society are undermined. Too much conservative rigidity and society stagnates.

Opening to insights from both extremes can lead to an important integration. A more radical and experimental approach to life can be seen as a way to free up life force from old pathways. Such an approach allows creativity, fluidity, and an expanded sense of identity. It encourages the emergence of the new, which is naturally more in the foreground with youth, who are at the experimental leading edge of our culture and are often drawn to wild celebrations that free up an ecstatic flow of energy.

The conservative value system offers a profound training in disciplining life force, mastering it with our will and channeling it along specific lines, which leads to greater societal order and stable values as well as enduring, effective, and profitable organizations. It also leads us to protect and preserve what is valuable.

These "trainings" each initiate something different in us. Ideally, we take on both trainings at some point in our lives so that we are able to be as full-spectrum as possible. If we don't embrace both ends of the spectrum, our highest potential may be compromised. For men, someone who remains attached to the unfettered flow of life force may fail to embrace traditional virtues of manhood. In California, we call them "flow boys." They crave freedom and fear commitment. They tend not to marry, and they often don't build much that endures, financially or organizationally. They retain a youthful delight in freedom without the adult commitments that build families, communities, and society. What they may lack in leadership they make up for in creativity, artistic ability, and innovativeness.

When we are young, with wide-open horizons, the more liberal perspective is typically at the foreground. Some level of rebellion against what we've inherited is a part of most people's natural maturation. However, as we take on increasing responsibilities and commitments, from marriage to family to organizations, we often need to discipline ourselves and focus on the preservation of society's structures through measured growth. We restrict our sexual expression to create a stable marriage; we dress appropriately to move in certain social circles; we build expertise in a more singular career; and we think more like an investor than a consumer. That's when the training in conservative virtues can be very helpful.

If denied, the more liberal orientation fails to free us from what is outdated, lopsided, and closed-minded in what we've inherited.

Overindulged, it keeps us from maturing into someone who can take responsibility for families, businesses, and communities.

So, one aspect of forging a sacred paradigm for America 7.0 is to respect the complementary balance between liberal and conservative worldviews. This respect can even be taken to another level, in which we consciously train with someone who is our opposite and learn to harness the power of that person's values and perspective on life. Such a stance ultimately reflects the view that we are all allies to each other on this planet and that we each have been endowed with characteristics that allow us to serve our function. To the extent that we accept our own values and respect the values of those with whom we differ, we can begin to work as a more cohesive and unified team on the largest challenges of our day.

I leaned heavily toward the experimental and liberal side of the equation in my twenties, even creating my first book with the title *Radical Spirit*. Its black and red cover spoke to this youthful rebellion against the old systems and structures. Many of its articles focused on the pioneering of experimental new spiritual pathways, some of which were quite edgy.

As I grew into my thirties, however, I began to experience the negative effects of being undisciplined: I burned some bridges with reckless truth telling and almost went broke on my first startup. At times, I destabilized my partnership with my eventual wife Devaa rather than supporting it to be secure and solid. It took these experiences to begin to see the wisdom of more conservative elders and the importance of balance and political cross-training. Based on a challenge from Devaa's father, who was much more conservative politically, I trained for two years in mixed martial arts to balance out the New Age flow boy in me with what he called "Stevie," more of a tough fighter. I took a mainstream job at an Internet company to learn the disciplines of business. I got myself on more sound footing fiscally. And I made a more rigorous commitment to my relationship with Devaa, eventually leading to a marriage that is the most cherished part of my life now.

As a CEO of a company now, I can savor the wild-eyed radical in me who loves to play at the experimental edge while also embracing the more measured, disciplined business leader that needs to be more conservative in certain decisions. I need both poles to do what I do effectively, and the same is true of most positions of real responsibility and leadership in our society, especially politics. To govern well and justly requires a level of respect for the status quo that youth tend not to have. It requires patience with the pace of change and an appreciation of incremental progress. This is not satisfying to those at the liberal extreme (and indeed it was not satisfying to me for many years). However, it is the result of balance, integrity, and maturity. I still count myself as a strong progressive, but one who now understands the wisdom held in conservative values; and I am more patient with the pace of our social evolution. I eventually released "radical" as my identity, which opened the way to seeing the world in a more sacred and inclusive way.

The simple truth is that life mastery requires versatility since different situations require different things. If we are only wildly creative, it's tough to plan for long-term organizational growth. And if we are only ultraconservative, we may miss the next innovation and creative movement that upends a market (or a world). Keeping a foot in both worlds lets us play outside the box while also understanding and respecting the rules of engagement on each side. It ultimately allows us to be integrated, wise, and effective leaders rather than people shouting slogans at the opposition.

6

Political Cross-Training

All partisan movements add to the fullness of
our understanding of society as a whole.
—Alice Walker

THE EVOLUTION OF AMERICA 7.0 will require all of us—not
just blue states or red states, but all states. Not just Democrats
but Republicans, Libertarians, and Greens. A major evolution of
our country requires the participation of vast numbers of Americans, at all levels of the political process. It will require a revitalized twenty-first century brand of citizenship that is informed,
empowered, and engaged. The biggest mistake we can make is to
expect that the Oval Office or Congress will do all the work, which
is a recipe for failure.

The first step for each of us in embodying greater political wisdom, which I started exploring in the last chapter, is to go beyond
exclusive polarities, even the polarity of change versus stability.
While the next evolution of America requires change, in seeking
that change, we are well served to honor the past upon which we
build. A conservative coworker once said to me, "The way I see it,
liberals are always trying to change things, and my job is to slow 'em
down." I found this an amusing way to see the dichotomy, as well as
speak to the deeper complementarity between value systems.

So while my temperament and values may be progressive, I find it helpful to practice embracing conservative values and seek the common ground that is the foundation of true progress. We can think of this as political cross-training, and it's a foundational principle for bringing a sacred dimension into our political process. We can also see this cross-training in the emerging field of transpartisanship, a wonderful movement that is gaining momentum and that approaches political divides with an attitude of civility, respect, and even curiosity, with a goal of finding more common ground.

The need for political cross-training and transpartisanship has grown quite dire because the level of partisanship has reached historic highs. In 1960, a poll that asked Americans whether they would be upset if their son or daughter married a member of the other political party found that only 5 percent of Republicans and 4 percent of Democrats would have. Fast-forward to 2010, and a YouGov poll found the same question resulted in 49 percent of Republicans and 33 percent of Democrats expressing concern over the prospect of intraparty marriage.[1] That level of polarization is clearly unhealthy for America.

My story of going beyond my own negative partisanship is to some extent every person's story as we seek to go beyond our natural predilections and honor values and perspectives that we don't naturally hold. In this chapter, I share more about my own journey into honoring conservative values. That honoring has not come easily. For the early part of my adulthood, I had a visceral disdain for the Republican Party and especially its most deeply conservative wing. They were the "force" holding us back and tethering us to the past, or so it seemed. And I felt annoyed by the power and influence they hold in our culture.

Eventually, rather than resenting conservatives' skill at amassing money and power, I began to think seriously about what I needed to learn from them. I studied the more conservative businessmen

I knew, listened to conservative pundits, undertook mixed martial arts training, and began to recognize that my "radical" identity was preventing me from accessing a more integrated, holistic, and balanced picture of myself. As I began to shift away from being exclusively a Radical Spirit, the brand I had adopted for my work, I joked that I was becoming a Mainstream Spirit. I was gradually embracing the more conservative values of respecting tradition, maintaining longer-term commitments, and building relationships, organizations, and activities in a stable fashion.

When I would give free rein to my desire for rapid change, I would undermine my ability to create enduring value. Manifesting something that endures, I learned, requires some wariness about excess change, a suspicion of the newest idea, and some skepticism about the value of the latest vision. It also requires commitment and focus over the long term. Conservative values often breed good businesspeople for this reason. There's a greater discernment about new ideas, which translates into more attention to detail, more commitment to staying the course, and a disciplined relationship with life—as well as a willingness and capacity to say no!

As I came to honor the conservative perspective on a deeper level, I began to see that conservatives more easily build upon a sense of lineage because they have greater respect for the past. They have more reverence for the power of a holy text like the Bible that has guided long epochs of human civilization. They have an abiding respect for what works in our market-driven economic system or the founding principles of our country. Conservatives also tend to feel more patriotic because they are more proud of our history and what we've already achieved. In that sense, they need not start from square one in their efforts, but stand on the shoulders of those who have gone before them.

Instead of critiquing the conservative viewpoint, I have learned to honor what I find beautiful about it. If we were to do this honoring collectively, it would help us to find a place of respect that transcends party lines by amplifying what is good rather than attempting to negate what is "wrong." When progressives fixate exclusively on the "problem" of conservatives, or vice versa, we polarize in a way that keeps us in a self-righteous and judgmental position. This entrenches us in our positions rather than opening us to greater wisdom.

I believe in doing everything we ethically can to champion the political candidates who represent our values and our highest vision. But we can do this from a ground of respect and honoring the so-called "other side." The truths we speak when we are truly honoring others' points of view will also be more easily received by people who don't share our predilections.

Ultimately, I see us all as divine beings carrying forward important tasks on planet earth. We may never understand the full story of why we are here and how we are serving these larger projects, or even with whom we are actually working in unseen realms. But I've seen enough to know that there is a grander plan that we are all co-creating. The more we can adopt a stance of respect and even love for the role of each of us in that plan, even those who might appear to be our antagonists, the more effective we can be in fulfilling our role.

For a progressive, it's a potentially liberating idea that, on a higher level, the most hated conservative "foe" may be our close collaborator in a larger plan. This person might be acting as a provocateur, offering an exaggerated viewpoint that causes us to evolve our own stance. And for a conservative, recognizing that a liberal activist might be part of the same spiritual team could be a breakthrough.

Political cross-training helps us to break out of our self-imposed boxes and see opinions, values, and policies with fresh eyes. If we don't engage this cross-training, we run the risk of wasting valuable energy on polarization, as well as inhibiting our own full development. Honoring what is foreign to us may run counter to our emotions and our personal histories as well as the encouragement of our social circles. It's easier to rehearse the litany of complaints and critiques we have about the "other." And yet so long as antagonism grows, we weaken our ability to work together toward shared goals or learn from the talents someone else has developed.

Political cross-training resembles sports cross-training; by training our body in different ways we can improve our skills in our "main" sport. Similarly, political cross-training says that we might become more effective progressives when we train and work with conservatives. Or that we may actually be a stronger conservative if we can spend time in an artist's colony and learn from their free-wheeling ways.

I'm thinking of my friend Joseph McCormick, who began his career as a military marksman, then graduated to opposition research for Republican candidates and even became a candidate for Congress from Georgia. After that phase of his life came to an end, he took a year in retreat in North Carolina in a rural area. Although he had held a strong visceral disdain for hippies from his youth, he met, befriended, and began to learn from his counter-cultural hippie neighbors. This was the genesis of a profound shift that eventually led him to create the Transpartisan Alliance to seek higher common ground and help reunite our democracy. His time "behind enemy lines" allowed him to grow and open in many ways, expanding the compass of his heart and leading him to a higher form of service than taking down Democratic candidates through his opposition research. Because he was respected by conserva-tives, Joseph was able to bring people like anti-tax activist Grover Norquist to the table with left-wing leaders such as Al Gore to engage in transpartisan dialogue.

While our personal stories might be less dramatic than Joseph's, they are no less important. How can we each truly learn from those who appear to hold opinions that are opposite ours?

My father-in-law Larry Mitchell was a man with strongly con-servative views. He initially had such disdain for my progressive views that we ended up in an email war that horrified my wife Devaa. After reading a column I wrote about Fierce Love as a response to terrorism, he took it upon himself to teach me a lesson—with many of his friends and family cc'd! During this intense exchange about the military, war, terrorism, and more, he blasted me with such gems as "If men are from Mars and women are from Venus, then Stephen is from Uranus." He was quite funny in his skewering at times (as well as brutal), but the initial paradigm clash eventually gave way to respect. I learned quite a bit from him, taking on his challenge to learn business disciplines and engage in mixed martial arts training to toughen up after years in more peaceful pursuits. In the end, he helped make a more balanced man out of me and provided me with some of my most significant political cross-training.

So ask yourself: Whom have I been judging? How might I take the time to learn from their perspectives and integrate their capacities? Doing this can make us all stronger and wiser citizens.

7

From Revolutionaries to Evolutionaries

A revolution is an idea which has found its bayonets.
—Napoleon Bonaparte

ON JULY 4 EVERY year, the skies of America light up with fire-works to commemorate the winning of the Revolutionary War for independence from England and the signing of the Declaration of Independence. For most of my adult life, I have frankly had mixed feelings about this holiday. While there is beauty in the patriotic joy, we tend to focus on the glory of winning a war rather than the enshrinement of sacred principles of liberty, equality, and justice for all. We do not make this a day of reconnecting and recommitting to our highest purpose. It is not a day for reflection, healing, or bridge-building. In short, it is not a day that we use to remember our country's higher purpose in a sincere way but instead to celebrate a war victory.

Taken to a deeper level, this is symbolic of another place where America needs to make a shift to truly fulfill our sacred purpose as a nation: growing from revolutionaries into evolutionaries. Revolutionaries are always engaged in a form of subtle or overt violence, as the Napoleon quote opening this chapter makes clear. Revolutionaries are attempting to overthrow someone or something, usually without respect for what has preceded them. There is a spirit of rebellion and antiestablishment quality in it.

For much of my younger adult life, I loved this revolutionary fire. What I increasingly came to see, though, is that revolutionary energy is a form of frozen development, stuck in late adolescence or early adulthood, rebelling against what we've inherited. There is a profound impatience at the core of revolution—a demand that whatever change we want is going to happen *now* and at whatever cost to life or limb.

A revolutionary tends to tilt toward megalomaniac tendencies. While holding onto noble ideals, there's a sense of arrogance about knowing better than everyone else and dismissing the validity in other positions to the point that we can even justify killing those who are in opposition. That's why political revolutions often lead to a changing of the leadership without a changing of the level of consciousness engaged—the same mess with different players.

An evolutionary is much more of a peaceful pilgrim, leading more patiently into new terrain, whether that is geographic, scientific, spiritual, political, or economic. An evolutionary may hold a strong mirror up to the status quo and work to end injustice but does so with more patience, respect, and nonviolence. Gandhi was an evolutionary, as were Martin Luther King Jr., Harriet Tubman, Susan B. Anthony, and Cesar Chavez.

An evolutionary is a builder, taking the given cultural foundation and growing it into the next form. He or she is invested in training successors, building capacity, and ensuring healthy societal structures to make sure positive changes endure. Evolutionaries often work behind the scenes and without ultimatums; they are interested in long-term results rather than short-term symbolism.

Revolutionaries have little of this patience. They enjoy big, dramatic flourishes of apparent heroism, often connected to personal glory. They tend to enjoy the adulation of being a winner. They love the intensity of struggle and the drama of warfare, whether physical or verbal. They draw energy from the fight. So when we celebrate the violent overthrow of the British each year on July 4, we are celebrating our early history as revolutionaries rather than our emerging role as evolutionaries. We are exalting the glory of battle over the more patient work of building.

For many years, I thought that America's Revolutionary War against Britain was a necessary and even laudable war. However, I've since been exposed to the insights of teachers who share that the higher intention of that time was to create a nonviolent separation of America from Britain that reflected the kind of healthy individuation we experience leaving our parents' homes, rather than the karma-creating violence of revolution. This perspective, which at first took me aback but then made perfect sense, is that the creation of the United States of America as a new template for civilization made our separation from Britain inevitable. However, the way in which we chose to separate from Britain was important. Would we do so with a natural, evolutionary, peaceful progression more akin to healthy individuation in adulthood? Or a violent rebellion?

That we chose the latter became the template for many later bloody revolutions, from the French Revolution to the Russian Revolution. By modeling revolutionary fire rather than evolutionary patience, our Founding Fathers unfortunately built excess violence into our vision of progress. The case can be made that this founding template of violent overthrow of the old became so central to American identity that it contributed to later wars such as the Civil War and continues to play out in the high rates of crime, violence, gun ownership, and incarceration today. In short, violent revolutionary qualities became glorified and memorialized, keeping us frozen in a more adolescent pattern as a country. Today, we still see ourselves as a country of revolutionaries and fail to understand that as a form of immaturity.

This reflection is not specific to either major political party, both of which take revolutionary qualities as part of their identity, from the countercultural hippies on the left to the Tea Party movement on the right. We saw the revolutionary fire playing out in the sixties as a large wave of change arose without adequate respect. "Don't trust anyone over thirty" was an apt motto for the revolutionary, young-adult fire. Rebel. Reject. Overthrow. While there was a wild explosion of creativity in the counterculture, it was also ungrounded because it lacked respect for the social structures and functions upon which the next evolution of America would have to build. On a basic level, this is why evolutionary movements are more successful than revolutionary ones.

I share these insights as relatively recent recognitions for me. As I have mentioned in previous chapters, I was hooked on the revolutionary fire in my twenties and early thirties. I loved the excitement of chaos and throwing caution to the wind. I experimented and pushed the envelope of freedom. And I still do enjoy some of that in moderation. However, my next level of growth required an equal embrace of responsibility hand in hand with freedom. We can only handle freedom to the extent that we take responsibility to manage its impacts. The sixties countercultural rebellion still had too much youthful fire in it to ground the changes long term. It actively rejected the wisdom of elders, conservatives, and straights. It was filled with its own rebellious hubris. And thus while it created fun festivals and grand gestures, many of its cultural experiments failed to come to fruition in the form of sustainable change—at least in the short term. The best leaders of the sixties went on to become evolutionaries, doing more inner work and taking on responsible societal roles. And only now are some of the cultural shifts they advocated for really coming to fruition.

My own journey of slowly becoming an evolutionary rather than a revolutionary is typical. It's also the journey of marrying liberal and conservative values, freedom with responsibility, change with stability. Just because we can see a potential future does not mean that the culture is ready to manifest it. Gordon Davidson, who coauthored

Spiritual Politics, likes to think about change on a five-hundred-year timescale. For a revolutionary, that's impossible: change needs to come *now*. However, for a true evolutionary, we recognize that the development of human beings and culture is a process that takes time to unfold. Some of the most valuable changes may take decades and even centuries. When we can work patiently toward outcomes that may not happen within our lifetime, that's when we know that we've become a reliable evolutionary.

Returning to our yearly celebration on July 4, what if we spent less time celebrating our revolutionary past and put more focus on our evolutionary future? What if we focused on what we can do together now to build a better America? What if we took time to heal the past, mature the American psyche, and unite as one people? This would help us move into the next stage of interdependence rather than just glorify our last big cultural shift into independence with explosives in the sky.

There's something a bit tragic about a high school sports hero who spends his time nostalgically remembering past victories rather than making something extraordinary of the present. In the same way, America cannot afford to rest on past "wins" but instead needs to focus that pioneering, evolutionary spirit on creating a still brighter tomorrow. This means letting go of some of the chest thumping and flag waving as well as the in-your-face revolutionary fire and the celebration of violence. The benefit is that we become a more enlightened, loving, and mature country that is a shining light for the world. We'll also be less prone to military campaigns that end up as long-term quagmires, which we've gotten stuck in from Vietnam to Afghanistan to Iraq.

Is that not worth letting go of some of our youthful fire?

8

Patriotism and Progress

We must love our country so deeply, and with such devotion, that our
internal "enemies" once again become fellow citizens, and perhaps one
day allies or even friends. The soul of our democracy depends on it.
—Mark Gerzon[1]

AFTER EXPLORING THE SHIFT from revolutionaries to evolutionaries, I want to reflect on the subject of patriotism and what I
think of as right relationship with our country.

Americans' love for our country is no small thing. We are willing
to die to protect our land. We glorify it in songs and heartfelt pledges
of allegiance. And we wear it with pride on our bumper stickers and
T-shirts. Political campaigns aim to harness that love and ride the
swell of emotion to victory.

While this dedication has a beautiful aspect, the limitation is
that the love behind much of today's patriotism can be blind and
unwilling to face the full truth of who we are. Constructive critiques
of our country's policies are often seen as unpatriotic rather than
as a legitimate expression of that same love. Speaking the straight
truth about our collective shadow can be received with outrage.

I thus believe it is time for our patriotism to evolve, which in
turn makes it easier for our country to evolve. When unquestioned
loyalty is mistaken for patriotism, we undermine the possibility of
our country progressing still further. True love is a force that calls

us to greater wholes—a bigger vision of ourselves, a more committed relationship, a nobler mission, or a deepened sense of compassion for others. Real love propels us forward. And that can require some toughness.

The teachers who have the biggest impact on our lives are likely not those who let us do whatever we want. The teachers who let us slack off tend to be popular but not truly influential. Influential teachers care deeply enough to challenge students with more expanded visions of themselves. They help their students stretch into greater maturity, expand their dreams, and encourage real excellence. Such teachers hold a bold picture of who we can become.

Patriotism based on flag waving and defending the status quo is a bit like the popular teacher. It is easy on us in the moment but undermining of our potential. What America's next stage of evolution requires is a deeper patriotism based upon a profound appreciation of the noble aspects of America's history and values that nonetheless does not shy away from facing the many ways we need to grow. Such patriotism begins to call forth our country's soul and turns the lock of our country's innermost secrets.

To evolve America, we do truly need to love it. But once we've established that loving relationship, we also need to champion the next greater, more mature version of our country. Even if we believe that we are the greatest country on earth, we are not nearly so great today as we can become tomorrow. That recognition is at the root of progress.

Conservatives tend to come down on the side of a patriotic pride that reinforces the status quo, ignores our shadow, and resists the next wave of change. This is a reflection of their important role in maintaining the best of our history but can result in idealization of that past.

Progressives, by contrast, often become fixated on critiques in a way that can diminish authentic respect for our successes in advancing a model for healthy democracy. While their critiques are rooted in the desire to achieve a better future, the disrespect can make the critiques taste too bitter and neglect important strengths that need to be honored. The critiques then backfire.

Both approaches hold us back from a relationship with our country that is based on a respectful love that looks unflinchingly at the truth of who we are—including all our failures, inadequacies, and problems—and calls us to our next, higher potential. The truth is that our country is quite young, a late adolescent among civilizations. In relationship to this young adult of a country, we can aspire to be like influential teachers—loving our country for what we have already achieved and how we have already served, while also calling us to still greater roles of leadership, service, honor, and creativity. That is when patriotism and progress can go hand in hand.

Part of this progress requires that we do some collective shadow work. In psychology, our shadow is the part of ourselves that we exclude from our current identity and thus are literally unable to see. Pride in our country can thus swell up in a way that makes it very difficult to see or face our American shadow.

Facing our shadow is also essential so we can clear out what is broken, misguided, or damaged from the last historical era before we attempt an upgrade. America's shadow side includes a lot of unfinished business of our many previous operating systems, which often thwarts and undermines our larger mission.

To do this shadow work, we need to look with clear eyes at some of the ways we've misused power, destroyed lives, and lived in partial truths about ourselves or our world. We need to face and own the ways that we have marginalized and victimized others, as well as do the work of healing, reparations, and reconciliation. We also need to look at the ways we have used violence as a tool of foreign policy and left behind badly damaged countries from Vietnam to Afghanistan to Iraq.

In looking at America's shadow side, it often contains the same qualities that can lead us to noble behaviors, but in immature and self-centered forms. Given the power we wield in the world, these places of immaturity have harmful effects on others and, ultimately, ourselves. Truth telling that is both rigorous and compassionate helps our shadow qualities come to the surface so they can evolve into their higher expression and thus alleviate any suffering they are now causing.

To get more specific, America has too often resembled a society of adolescents, more concerned with building our own status, comfort, and power than leaving a legacy of service. We have feasted on the riches of the world as the biggest consumers on the planet while the global environment deteriorates. We have thrown our weight around on the world stage, often without respect for other countries. We have undermined significant global accords and treaties if they put any constraints on our behavior. We profess to be a generous country and yet we give a smaller percentage of our GDP to overseas development than other major developed economies—only .19 percent of our gross national income, which puts us in nineteenth place.[2]

We are, in short, overly impressed with our virtues and often unapologetic about our vices. The "ugly American" reputation overseas is rooted in a sense of entitlement that others should learn our language and play by our rules—even in their own land. We intuit the greatness of our mission but overestimate the degree to which we've achieved it. So the question becomes, why are we stuck in this way? Are we simply too young as a country to behave with greater maturity? Or is there something deeper going on, something that can be remedied?

A basic principle in psychology is that when we have a traumatic experience that we don't want to feel, part of us contracts. We hold our breath, move away from the pain, or hold the negative memories in our unconscious. We continue moving forward, but a part of us remains stuck in a time warp. Often this results in a compulsion to repeat: the abused little girl finds herself in one abusive relationship after another, or the abandoned boy is left by his wife as an adult. The psychological motive in this repetition is to recreate a version of the original experience in order to bring the old wounds to the surface. If we are able to face this process consciously, we can heal, and effectively clear the past. If not, we create another round of repetition.

Our national psychology can be seen as having parallels to an individual's. We have enduring memories that are passed down to the next generation, as well as core beliefs, values, and stories about who we are. This American psyche shapes us through education, entertainment, cultural stories, and shared value systems. It is mirrored in the kind of leaders we choose and the decisions we make.

Looking at America's psychology with this lens leads us to address the root causes of less mature behaviors in our national consciousness. Where have we become stuck as a country? What experiences have we not wanted to fully feel? What is incomplete in our history that needs to be remedied and released? Where are parts of our culture still traumatized? These questions lead us into parts of our national history where we have not been truthful with ourselves and where we have not been willing to take full responsibility for the consequences of our actions. America's darker moments in the past feed the shadows of our present. Merely switching parties in power does not heal the distortions or clear the history that is keeping America in a cycle of less-than-noble behaviors. This collective shadow work is part of the journey that we need to undertake as a country to become more healthy and whole, as well as to deliver on the extraordinary potential activated in our founding vision. This is the journey of deep patriotism that calls us to a higher level of our greatness. In the next chapters we'll explore a few aspects of our national shadow and how we can begin to heal them collectively.

9

Reconnecting with Indigenous Roots

Humankind has not woven the web of life. We are but one thread within it. Whatever we do to the web, we do to ourselves. All things are bound together. All things connect.
—Chief Seattle

IN THE LAST CHAPTER, I set the context for why America needs to delve deeper into our shadow and our history to clear patterns that are blocking us from going to the next level. Many of these patterns have roots in the misuse of power. Our founding philosophy champions "inalienable" rights, but the way in which we have wielded power often does not reflect that philosophy. To understand this gap between our ideals and our embodiment of those ideals, we need to start very early in our history.

The first historical fact that has been written about by many but which we as a nation have never adequately faced, understood, and integrated is the fact that we are a country founded on genocide. We celebrate the history of our Founding Fathers and forget that they were living on land taken from decimated peoples. The continent that Europeans "discovered" had a long history of settlement, with a great diversity of societies. In 1492, there were an estimated ten to eighteen million Indigenous people north of Mexico.[1]

Many of these societies had sophisticated cultures, mature philosophies, and even advanced systems of government. Some met the European invaders with generosity that was often then exploited. Others fought back, which hastened their demise. After a few hundred years of conquest and disease, less than one million Native Americans remained.

Let that fact sink in: America was founded on a Native American genocide larger than that of Hitler's genocide of the Jews (six million killed). This historical fact, when squarely faced, explains a great deal about why our country's heart is not fully open, why we are prone to arrogance, and why we struggle to live in harmonious ways. It is a massive wound that has never truly healed. We have not addressed the damage, worked toward reconciliation, and learned the deeper lessons about power this experience could teach us. The avoidance of that process keeps us in an overly rosy vision of our country.

To wield power in a healthy way means going beyond the psychology of perpetrators and victims, winners and losers, oppressors and oppressed. The key to doing so is acknowledging both the oppressor and the oppressed in us. If we see the criminal in us as well as the victim, we can act with more wisdom and self-awareness. If we do not see ourselves in both, we become lopsided and thus potentially dangerous, especially as we wield vast power on the world stage.

Americans tend to sculpt a view of our history that concentrates on our liberation of the oppressed, such as liberation from England ("no taxation without representation"), liberation from Europe's religious strictures, and liberation from state-controlled economies through capitalism. We see ourselves as the redeemer of the victim and the champion of the downtrodden. Our great rallying call of freedom similarly speaks to the liberation of the oppressed. And it is undeniably true about America that in many cases we have acted as a liberator, such as our noble defense of Europe in World War II.

Identifying ourselves primarily with this positive side, however, means that we have a challenging time seeing ourselves as oppressors. We have an allergic reaction to evidence that we are in the wrong. We are innovators, healers, and liberators, not empire builders, exploiters, and colonialists, right? The truth is that we are both.

Our Native American genocide is significant for the psychology of our country because it was our foundational example of being the oppressors. It is our first template of the destructive use of power in which our ancestors invaded the land of other people, disrespected them, killed them, and took it for their own. In refusing to experience the horror of what our ancestors perpetrated on the native peoples of this land, we become blind to seeing ourselves today as oppressors. Our denied shadow is thus acted out unconsciously.

Facing America's original genocide and doing the work of reconciliation with Indigenous peoples is one of the important keys to unlock the door to a mature relationship with our power. It will also open us to a deeper connection to the land on which we live. So long as we ignore the wound in our relationship with this land, we tend to live in unsustainable, ungrounded, and disrespectful ways. We are literally unable to activate our roots.

The work of healing our original genocide can also reconnect our culture as a whole with native lineages, which offer important wisdom for our present time and could have a more prominent role in our country's vision for the future. Indeed, scholars have revealed just how significantly the Founding Fathers drew from the Iroquois Confederacy as a template for our system of governance. In this sense, our democratic heritage draws as strongly from native people's principles and ideals as from European Enlightenment thinkers. Equally important as what was copied from the Iroquois model is what was not: for example, clan mothers chose the representing chiefs, or *sachems*, on the Grand Council and could remove them as well, thus providing a key element of gender balance in government, which was not included in the founding government of America.

Indigenous peoples have lived far longer on this land than European settlers and have wisdom to share about how to do so in harmonious ways. Many Indigenous peoples have been raised with a profound appreciation for the sacredness of the earth and all its inhabitants, which leads to a natural desire to more carefully steward our resources. Their cultural history is often based on putting the community first, a practice we need more of in our hyper-individualistic nation.

Native American rituals also have a transformative power to lift us beyond limited views of ourselves and find a higher vision. The Sun Dance ceremony of the Plains tribes, for example, leads participants to transcend their limits of pain with days of dancing, deprivation, and intense body piercing, all to discover their connection to Creator and offer themselves for service.

In many ways, Indigenous wisdom can help us apply sacred values such as oneness, respect, and love if we are simply open to listen and learn. I have participated in several sweat lodges, for example, which play an important role in Indigenous tradition. Sitting shoulder-to-shoulder in a sweltering lodge, we learn to sing in community and endure hardship with love. We offer prayers and blessings to our Creator, learn to lean on each other for support, cleanse ourselves of illusion, and commit to greater purity. A sweat brings our bodies into deep relationship with the elements—earth, water, air, and fire. We are moved from ideas about Spirit into prayerful supplication, beginning with those who are least well-off in our world and only in the end returning to ourselves. I have grown from this exposure, which has balanced my own upbringing and strengthened my connection to our land.

Walking a sincere path of reconciliation with Native Americans can help to curb our current arrogance and bring our feet into deeper contact with the soil of this continent. Arrogance often compensates for a deeper feeling of inadequacy and lack of grounding. America's shadow side of arrogance reflects our recognition of a powerful destiny, followed by an attempt to inflate into that role before we've matured into it. To wield power in a sacred way requires humility, which in turn comes from respect for what has come before us.

Facing our original genocide requires a humbling of our national ego, which can be painful but redemptive. Germany, for instance, has become a mature, healthy, and prosperous country—productive, democratic, and socially conscious. It helped to advance the creation of the European Union even though it once provoked the bloodiest wars. It has matured by facing the shadow side of its impulse toward "greatness"—which manifested in the urge to dominate the world and create a master race, eliminating those who did not fit that vision. Its initiation into adulthood as a country came through the devastation of World War II. The country was destroyed, humbled, and humiliated, which eventually led to something more noble, mature, and generous to emerge.

I believe that we can face our own history with an open heart and do what it takes to heal the past and establish right relationship with the peoples our ancestors have harmed. This could take the form of a National Day of Reconciliation and Honoring. Or a national apology. Or Chautauqua-like tours offering a unique integration of native and Western cultures. Or, more substantively, the creation of an Indigenous Council of America, which could offer native peoples a pathway to wield actual power through our political system.

Focusing on forward-looking solutions that harness the best Indigenous wisdom can help us avoid the "guilt-trap" where we just feel badly about the past without taking positive steps forward. The point is not to wallow but to officially and deeply acknowledge the history, take on the work of healing, and make sincere strides toward creating solutions to current challenges, including the devastating rates of poverty, addiction, and poor health on reservations.

It is valuable to note here that in many Indigenous lineages there is a prophecy that we have entered the era in which Indigenous and white people will come back into sacred relationship with each other. Our South American brothers and sisters foresee the reunification of the Eagle and the Condor. When they fly together again, these prophecies share, we will have harmony. Similarly, the Hopi have prophesied this time as one in which the four major tribes on planet earth come back into circle together. Each has stewarded a different element: the black tribes have stewarded water, the yellow tribes air, the white tribes fire, and the Indigenous tribes earth. As we come back into respectful relationship with each other, the Sacred Hoop is restored and we bring balance and harmony to our world.

I see beautiful things emerging from this re-honoring. I have had a vision of representative leadership of America's Indigenous peoples joining in sacred ceremony with our current political leadership. Imagine such a ritual on the Washington Mall, with leaders from the House, the Senate, and even the president joined in ceremonial circle with the elders of our Indigenous peoples. The repercussions of meeting in such a way would help to heal hundreds of years of dishonor. Such a bridge-building would not merely be about clearing the past but about mutual learning in the present. The very qualities of arrogance and corruption that we often lament in our politicians are ones that could be balanced by the humility, sincerity, and groundedness that is evident in many of the leaders of Indigenous peoples, who built a requirement for humility into their selection process for leaders.

Our governing culture has been created mostly out of the values of white European culture, which means, from the Hopi perspective, that we have excess fire in our national psyche, leading to a propensity for war, competition, violence, arrogance, and inflation.

Reconnecting with the wisdom of Indigenous peoples can temper that fire, balancing it with the earth element that runs more strongly in their cultural DNA. The root of humility comes from the Latin root *humus*, meaning ground. As we connect with the earth element through Indigenous allies, we learn how to temper our aggression and reconnect with wholeness. So it is not merely a nice idea to do this work to heal the past; it's in many ways a prerequisite for a more truly evolved America 7.0.

Each of us can take this work on in our unique way: personal study, ritual circles, friendships, economic development on reservations, or advocating for a national day of reconciliation. Whatever our contribution is, it's simply a matter of making a commitment to be part of the healing and then listening for the best way that we can each do our part. When our intention is sincere, many opportunities emerge for how to fulfill it.

I will share a bit about my own work in this area. In 2012, my company The Shift Network joined forces to craft a Declaration of Commitment to Indigenous Peoples—a pledge of supportive partnership in addition to apologies for the past. More than ten thousand people joined in signing this document online before it was offered to members of the International Council of Thirteen Indigenous Grandmothers.[2] We also partnered with the grandmothers on virtual teaching work that helped spread their message throughout the world.

In 2014, we partnered with Chief Phil Lane Jr., a prominent leader from Canada, for a Global Indigenous Wisdom Summit, which built more bridges of sincere trust and respect. This led to another opportunity for partnership when there was a sudden need for emergency funds for Indigenous leaders to convene at the Summit of the Americas at which Western heads of state gather. The government of Panama had, at the last minute, pulled back its commitment to fund the parallel Indigenous Summit. The $65,000 we raised from over eight hundred donors in forty countries in five days provided not only the money necessary to have the meetings but also a real sense of partnership, respect, and healing.

In 2015, we were also called upon to support a vision of Jean Fleury to have the 125th anniversary of the Wounded Knee Massacre on December 29 be a date that supports the work of ending massacres worldwide. A sacred ceremony marked the culmination of an eight-day ride on horseback by the Reunion Riders, who retraced the trail of their ancestors through South Dakota's bitter cold. For the actual ceremony, people gathered in more than one hundred other sites around the world, to pray, heal, and commit to ending war and massacre.

Looking forward, we will continue to support the fulfillment of the prophecies of the reunification of the tribal peoples of the Americas and partner with them to influence the larger world toward a lasting peace. While the wounds of genocide are too vast to address with any one action, each bridge built is another opportunity for healing and coming into wholeness. As we each take small steps, we reweave the threads of wisdom that Indigenous peoples carry back into the fabric of our American culture. As we do this work, which was left incomplete at our founding, we create a more whole, compassionate, and loving foundation on which to build America 7.0.

Healing the Legacy of Slavery

Darkness cannot drive out darkness; only light can do that.
Hate cannot drive out hate; only love can do that.
—Martin Luther King Jr.

WITH THE ELECTION OF Barack Obama as president, we crossed an important threshold in our journey beyond racism. We cannot underestimate the long-term effect of having America's first family be African American for eight years. Even if we don't support President Obama's policies or job performance, his presence in the Oval Office reflected a long march beyond slavery and accelerated the day that the final color barriers drop.

Nonetheless, the rifts and wounds from the era of deep inequality for African Americans are still in place, in both black- and white-skinned citizens. The true legacy of slavery lies in the heart of all of us, including in our subconscious mind, where so many split-second decisions are made, from gauging whether someone is dangerous to deciding if we'd want to hire a person for a job. In the years ahead, it is up to each of us to acknowledge and cleanse that residue and enter the new era of real diversity wholeheartedly. Disrespect, unequal opportunity, racism, injustice, and police brutality toward African Americans are still a festering wound in our culture. We have a lot of work to do in the years ahead to heal the past and forge a new future by eliminating discrimination, as well as by building bridges of love and understanding between races.

The pathway to increased understanding requires social healing on a large scale. It involves listening to each other, being present to pain, and exploring ways to resolve negative memories and reveal hidden power dynamics. It also involves working together in practical ways on shared social issues such as injustice in the criminal justice system as well as creating more economic opportunity, which Martin Luther King Jr. turned his focus to in the last years of his ministry.

I believe it is beholden upon non-black people to be partners in this cultural healing and really go beyond comforting platitudes to facing the core of suffering, separation, and racism. The gifts that will open in this process are not just for Americans but for the world. Indeed, they can reconnect all of us with our ancestral human roots in Africa, a continent that bears the scars of exploitation as no other does. In the end, we are all Africans, since we all trace our ancestry to this mother continent. To live and breathe as one global people, we need something akin to an African family reunion, one in which we honor the shared heritage of all races and peoples. Fully facing America's history around African enslavement is part of redeeming our relationship with African peoples, which goes beyond the paternalism of philanthropy to a stance of partnership and respect. African culture is our mother culture, quite literally, and we have not honored our mother.

Indeed, American culture *is* African culture if we trace the roots back far enough into prehistoric times. And even in recent times, African American culture has infused American culture with spiritual depth and moral clarity, with inspired music and evolutionary religious movements, with great literature and profitable enterprises, and with creating thinking and innovative entertainment. African American preachers, musicians, activists, and innovators have been at the forefront of every major American cultural evolution. In short, African Americans have been one of the great catalysts for the growth of America and will be key players in the next evolution of our country. Healing America's history with black Americans can connect us with the great joy, appreciation, and connection that live so vividly in the African American community.

It's heartening that in recent years we've seen more breakthroughs in the political arena, from the 2015 surge of presidential candidate Ben Carson to the forefront of the Republican field to young black senators like Cory Booker and Tim Scott. And it's also interesting that the entertainment industry is starting to support this shift by honoring black leadership more: one of our most popular TV shows, *Scandal*, now features a powerful black female protagonist named Olivia Pope at the highest levels of Washington power. In 2015, Viola Davis became the first African American woman to win an Emmy for best actress in a drama. We're also looking with sober eyes at our history, as in recent years we've seen the searingly important drama of *12 Years a Slave* win the Best Picture Oscar along with the release of a powerful retelling of Martin Luther King Jr.'s story in *Selma*.

While there are some positive signs like these of moving beyond our ugly racial history, the challenges are still large. The rates of incarceration for African American men are intolerably high, with one in three born today facing imprisonment at some point in their lives.[1] And the rate of poverty among African American children remains at an unconscionable level of almost 40 percent.[2]

Discrimination and unwarranted violence by police against our black citizens have sparked massive protests, movements, and soul-searching in recent years from Ferguson to Baltimore. These events pull the scab off the wounds of the era of legally sanctioned discrimination. Unhealed wounds and subterranean prejudice still erode African Americans' self-esteem, career opportunities, and sense of inclusion, which then feeds into a cycle of poverty and diminished opportunities. The solution begins with each of us building bridges of connection and understanding, as well as championing education and opportunities that prepare more African Americans to be on an equal footing. And it also means getting more serious about uplifting the poor in our country, with better jobs, health care, and education.

Some of the most inspiring initiatives to me in this area have been founded by Van Jones, who has activated multiple organizations and movements that are uplifting communities of color and healing America's opportunity divide. From the Ella Baker Center for Human Rights, which focuses on issues of criminal justice and incarceration, to Green for All, which has championed green jobs as a pathway out of poverty, to campaigns such as #YesWeCode and #cut50, Van has blazed a trail of pragmatic, forward-looking initiatives that make a real impact. #YesWeCode is a national initiative focused on empowering one hundred thousand low-opportunity youth to become software programmers. #cut50 is a remarkable bipartisan initiative launched with Republican Newt Gingrich to cut our prison populations in half. Part of the bipartisan logic of this initiative is that lower rates of incarceration are valuable to both progressives and conservatives for different reasons. Progressives tend to focus more on issues of racial justice whereas conservatives want to cut the size and expense of government. Together, they can find common ground in a goal of harnessing all the strategies available to reduce our incarceration rates closer to the rest of the developed world. Van has a knack for forging bold ideas that are inclusive and innovative and enrolling many other leaders in moving them forward.[3] These sorts of initiatives, which focus on enhanced opportunity for all, offer a great way to create positive momentum going forward.

The internal and interpersonal work of healing racial divides is also essential. I participated in one promising event in 2013 called "A National Conversation on Race: Walking Each Other Home" in Vallejo, California, which is statistically the most diverse city in our country[4]. The event featured LeVar Burton, the actor who broke new ground as Kunta Kinte in the miniseries *Roots*, followed by a workshop with Lee Mun Wah of StirFry Seminars and Aliah Majon, two people who have pioneered innovative diversity work. What they demonstrated in the workshop is that deep dialogue about our racial biases and perspectives can be edgy, revealing, and ultimately healing, provided we have a real commitment to do our work and create a safe container to do so.

At The Shift Network, this has not yet become one of our primary areas for contribution, but we have started to make some progress with our first online African American Wisdom Summit during Black History Month in February 2016. We've built bridges to some key communities of color with our Peace Ambassador Training, bringing it to over eighty community peacebuilders in Oakland and Detroit, and our 2011 Summer of Peace launch event in Oakland was one of our largest and most diverse public events. We also hosted our Birth 2012 event at Agape International, which is a wonderfully diverse spiritual community led by Michael Bernard Beckwith and Rickie Byars Beckwith in Southern California. On the personal front, my wife Devaa has also been involved for many years in a theater program at San Quentin State Prison that serves many black inmates, which has been a catalyst for growth, racial healing, and self-expression. We've also hosted a fundraiser at our house for a Green Youth Arts and Media Center in Oakland, which focuses on at-risk youth from communities of color.

While this is a start, I recognize that there is still much more to do. It's vital that we build bridges of understanding both to activist movements like Black Lives Matter that are seeking an end to racially based police violence and to police officers on the other side, who can feel compromised in their ability to protect people and perform a very hard job. Since the schism is particularly deep between African American communities and police, it can be particularly important for all of us who can to hold the ground of compassionate understanding of all sides while recognizing that we are both part of the solution and often unconsciously part of the problem.

Issues of racial justice also cannot be separated from economic issues. On the deepest level, America 7.0 will need to have a better economic design that keeps more people more gainfully employed at fair wages, something we'll explore a bit later. This will disproportionately help black people and Native Americans, who have the highest rates of poverty of any of our minority populations.

More than anything else, I believe that we ultimately need to embrace each other as family across the lines of race and do what we are each guided to do to heal the wounds, erase the old divides, and create a country of equal opportunity for all. Whether that means attending a black church or engaging in a racial healing dialogue or hiring a black staff member or reaching out to make more friends, we all have our role to play. America's sacred destiny cannot be fulfilled so long as our black citizens continue to suffer so much marginalization. It's time for us to heal the lingering legacy of slavery at last.

Rebalancing Feminine
and Masculine

*Because man and woman are the complement of one
another, we need woman's thought in national affairs to
make a safe and stable government.*
—Elizabeth Cady Stanton

WE NEXT TURN OUR attention to healing the relationship between masculine and feminine. The rebalancing of gender is really at the heart of creating a healthy and high-functioning American democracy. That's because the vast majority of new life on our planet comes from the union of masculine and feminine. This dynamic drives evolution itself—the combination of a polarity into a new unity, which unleashes our innate creative power. We thus create best when masculine and feminine are engaged in a joyful, even ecstatic dance of co-creation. This is not limited to the biological level of sex. Visionary author Barbara Marx Hubbard has coined the term *suprasex* to describe how two people can join their higher genius in a way that has similar excitement but that produces fruit in the form of creative gifts for the world. Suprasex applies to our higher needs and the achievement of our grandest visions.[1]

A sacred America is one in which masculine and feminine energies have found a deep and abiding balance with each other—as well as within each of us—a mutual honoring that results in harmony, love, and creativity. Just as a strong partnership creates a foundation for a family, so does a balance between masculine and feminine qualities result in a healthy and whole country.

For our entire history to date, masculine values, perspectives, and virtues have predominated. We are a nation founded by men, and our history has caused masculine virtues and values to become synonymous with America. Our celebration of independence, self-reliance, competition, and winning all tend to privilege masculine qualities over feminine. Though women have played a vital role at all stages of our country's cultural evolution, it is only recently that women have begun occupying seats of power in sufficient number to start to rebalance our national character.

In many traditional cultures, women are considered the natural gatekeepers for the sacred. Their ability to birth new life and to nurture that life into maturity is seen as placing them closer to the Divine. Women's tendency to strengthen relationships and collaborations is similarly related to the sacred value of oneness. By making oneness a lived reality, women bring our society into alignment with a foundational spiritual truth. On a subtler level, "women's intuition" has traditionally given women more openness to higher guidance and inspiration. In ancient times, this led them to play the role of priestess or oracle—bringing wisdom into the earth plane. In many ways, women are thus more connected to the depth dimension of life.

I have found myself drawn to a number of extraordinary women teachers and healers, including my wife Devaa and circles that she has helped to create. I was fortunate to participate in such a circle as one of only two men. While I ultimately found that my style of moving in the world is more masculine, which led me into men's circles and eventually men's initiations, I also found great appreciation for the spirited, freeform, embodied way in which women connect through song, sharing, movement, and ritual. By forging circles of support, these women are revalidating and redis-covering the sacred feminine in their lives and then bringing that more fully into the world through organizations, healing work, businesses, and even politics.

We have made quite extraordinary strides in the cause of women's rights in the last hundred years, but we still have a long way to go to true gender balance in our society, which runs deeper than simply having women in positions of power. Gender bal-ance requires a profound respect for feminine values and quali-ties of being, which can be present in both men and women. If we place women in positions of power who have largely abandoned feminine qualities to reach those positions, the goal of achieving a healthy balance in our society remains out of reach.

When women and men are able to embrace masculine and feminine qualities on an equal footing, both in themselves and in our society, we will have the recipe for a truly sacred America. The reason for this is simple: if masculine and feminine are equally required for creation, they both need to be operating in an optimal way for us to birth our most magnificent creations. Respect, appre-ciation, and even mutual reverence allow our masculine and femi-nine qualities to reach their highest expression. If one is diminished or disempowered in relationship to the other, it will necessarily undermine the quality of the "child" of that union.

A key point here is that masculine and feminine qualities exist in both men and women. Our recent cultural struggle over the marital rights of gays and lesbians brought this issue to the fore-ground, since masculine and feminine qualities exist in different proportions and combinations in the LGBT community than in the conventional definitions of man and woman. This gender com-plexity can be threatening to those holding more traditional views; however, embracing this is a vital part of rebalancing masculine and feminine values in our culture. When we accept a more fluid relationship between masculine and feminine qualities, which can express in many kinds of love, from sexual intimacy to marriage to social co-creation, we are en route to creating an America that is gender balanced.

Our ability to honor gay Americans with the rights and respect accorded to all Americans is thus a barometer of how much progress we have made in balancing masculine and feminine values in ourselves and our culture. When both sides of the polarity are respected and honored, in both men and women, it's emotionally far easier to allow for a fluidity of expression as befits our natural predilections. As we each find our own natural set point, we can engage the co-creative dance of masculine and feminine qualities in whatever personal and professional configurations feel most aligned—male/male, female/male, female/female. Ultimately, gender freedom is interwoven with our spiritual liberation. If we are only able to embrace one side of the polarity, we cannot be enlightened and free. Our true liberation requires the embrace of the full spectrum of life, and if we can only identify with half we will remain lopsided and subtly trapped.

On a practical political level, it is time for both men and women to champion a dramatic increase in the number of women in positions of political power. And not simply women in pantsuits who can slug it out with the good old boys; we need female political leaders (as well as male) who are unabashed in their embrace of feminine qualities so that those qualities can reshape the political landscape of our country.

What if we started a campaign to elect 50 percent women at all levels of power and in all parts of the country? Currently in the 114th Congress, women constitute just under 20 percent of our senators and representatives, which virtually assures an imbalance of masculine and feminine qualities at the level of our national decision-making.[2]

When Justin Trudeau became Canada's prime minister in 2015, he appointed a cabinet that was exactly 50 percent female and 50 percent male, which set off a wave of excitement around the world. It reflected the hunger in all of us to see our human diversity reflected in our political leadership.

A vast increase in elected women officials would result in a sea change in the political culture, something championed by bestselling author and founder of the Sister Giant movement, Marianne Williamson. Susan B. Anthony said, "There never will be complete equality until women themselves help to make laws and elect lawmakers." As our planet reels under the damage we are doing, political leaders with more feminine energy can stir our compassion, open our hearts, and rebalance our priorities on a global scale.

It's important to bear in mind that the feminine is not only soft and gentle; it can also be fiercely protective. Marianne Williamson often speaks about the importance of the "mother bear" quality in women that protects the undefended; when her cubs are threatened it evokes a ferocious level of protectiveness. This mother bear quality is now sorely needed to protect our planet and champion the disadvantaged. So part of embracing women in power is to value this aspect as well.

With so much wealth and power held in men's hands, I believe it's vital that more men dedicate themselves to the cause of feminine leadership in the world, perhaps bracketing our own desires for power to support women to step into roles historically occupied by men. I have done this with quite a number of women in my life, from authors to political leaders. Seeing women shine and step into their full power has been a blessing in itself, and I feel like it has benefited me as a man as well. There is nothing as beautiful as a powerful woman who honors and loves you. In Hinduism, it is said that the goddess of prosperity Lakshmi pours her abundance on those who revere her. When we revere the feminine in the world, we men receive a great blessing from the feminine in return, which in turn allows a more full-spectrum masculine power to emerge in us.

On a personal level, it is perhaps obvious that men need to celebrate career-advancement and pay equality for women, as well as shoulder our share of the work of family and home so that more women feel they have the space and support to step into public forms of leadership. I also think it is important to encourage women to pursue big dreams, including holding public office, running companies, or standing as top experts in their domain, as well as holding roles as religious and spiritual leaders. Often the glass ceilings these days are psychological as much as literal. Having the enthusiastic support of men who champion feminine leadership can be an important gift for our wives, friends, and allies, in addition to the many ways women are already empowering each other.

A further step beyond female political leadership will be to elect more openly lesbian, gay, bisexual, and even transgender politicians. The 2009 movie *Milk* offered a powerful depiction of the first man to overcome centuries of discrimination and become an openly gay politician. Harvey Milk's story was a breakthrough, and his legacy continues with a growing number of openly gay political leaders throughout our country, including in normally conservative states such as Utah and Texas. Their election represents one of the final fronts in rebalancing our national character and honoring masculine and feminine qualities at a political level. A remarkable example is Houston, which in 2009 was the largest city to elect an openly gay mayor, even though it is in a more traditionally conservative area. It was noteworthy that Mayor Annise Parker did not make gay rights a foreground issue for her administration but rather focused on the job of being a great mayor. This bodes well for a new era in which sexual orientation fades into the background as just one aspect of our humanness that is accepted and embraced.

In 1886, France sent a beautiful token of its friendship in the form of the Statue of Liberty, which occupies a cherished place in our national symbolism. More than one hundred million US citizens have ancestors who passed beneath the welcoming gaze of this statue built to honor the United States' commitment to ending slavery. Her torch burns for liberty for all. Visiting her is a poignant testimony to the sacred heart of America that has welcomed the oppressed, marginalized, and downtrodden from around the world to begin a new life. The poem penned by Emma Lazarus that was eventually inscribed on Lady Liberty says, "Give me your tired, your poor, / Your huddled masses yearning to breathe free . . ." This is the compassionate voice of the Mother, the powerful, all-embracing feminine that has spent too long in the shadows of American power. This is the voice we need to listen to when debating taking in refugees.

Her embrace of the most oppressed among us reminds us of the sweet face of the Goddess—all-loving and all-caring. It's a face of the Divine that is personal, protective, and welcoming to all. Bringing back this feminine face of the Divine is essential for us to find the wholeness that is part of our sacred code. That is why the Statue of Liberty is on the front of this book; she represents an era in which the feminine finds her rightful and co-equal partnership with the masculine at the heart of American power. It is time. And that single shift, perhaps more than any other, can ensure we fulfill our sacred mission and create a world that truly works for all.

Occupy the 100 Percent

*The purpose of life is undoubtedly to know oneself. We cannot do it
unless we learn to identify ourselves with all that lives.*
—Mohandas Gandhi

IN THE FALL OF 2011, the Occupy movement erupted onto the
global stage, spreading like wildfire from New York's Zuccotti
Park to locations around the world. The sheer speed of this growth
led to a great deal of excitement about its potential. While its ultimate objectives were not well articulated, one slogan came to cap-
ture its spirit: "We are the 99 percent." This slogan served as a
powerful statement that the 1 percent elite of the world cannot
shape our society solely in a way that serves only their interest.

Defying early attempts to pigeonhole it into a simple, misguided, or anarchic protest movement, Occupy quickly grew into
a resilient, mostly leaderless movement without clear demands
but with an egalitarian spirit, some fascinating methods of organizing, and high visibility. The movement's core message brought
attention to rising economic inequality and the subversion of our
democracy by corporations and elites. This is essential work, for
these inequalities have become barriers to the evolution of our
world and the fulfillment of our higher purpose.

The Occupy movement offered us both deep inspiration regarding the power of individuals to stand up while also offering cautions. Perhaps most problematic was the slogan itself that proved so catchy and enduring, "We are the 99 percent." The strategy of building an identity for the 99 percent who are opposed to the 1 percent creates a rift in the human family. Rather than reuniting us under the banner of the 100 percent, the 99 percent become polarized against the 1 percent, something that has fueled many violent revolutions in the past. When we are the 99 percent pitted against the 1 percent, we are in a family feud filled with anger. Anger can be an effective motivational tool at times, but it's a poor daily practice since it tends to disconnect us from our higher wisdom, deeper love, and the potential for mutual support. It focuses us on outer blame and neglects inner change. Anger is better at creating righteous "victims" than proactive solutions; it leaves polarization and resentment in its wake rather than wholeness and collaboration. The 1 percent begins to feel frightened and the 99 percent feels outraged rather than all of us seeing the ways our choices and actions contribute to unfair systems. The higher calling is for us to occupy the 100 percent—to see ourselves in all parties.

From the beginning of the movement it was clear to me that I am both the 99 percent and the 1 percent in a literal way. Growing up middle class with parents who both worked for public institutions, I had always lived close to the edge financially. I had almost gone broke several times and never even had a savings account as an adult until I was thirty-nine. So I could identify with the 99 percent and was personally aware of some of the injustices of a system that heavily favors the rich. On the other hand, as a graduate of Stanford and recent owner of a growing startup, I also recognized myself in the 1 percent, the elites of the capitalist system. And beyond any actual ups and downs in my economic "ranking," there is the deeper truth that I have friends who live on the economic edge, living month to month, and others who live in opulence, allies who are frontline protestors and others who are multimillionaires. I truly have a foot in both worlds.

My wife Devaa and I decided to embrace both identities over Thanksgiving weekend in 2011 while visiting her family in Los Angeles. We purchased a bag of groceries to distribute to protestors and brought our tents and sleeping bags to sleep in the Occupy Los Angeles encampment on the lawn of City Hall. While there, we met some fascinating people, such as a joyful man from Africa who had once been tortured in his country, escaped as a refugee, and had become a pilot in the United States, achieving a measure of middle-class success. But then the recession cost him his job and eventually his home. He now cheerfully staffed the volunteer table, recognizing the importance of the land of opportunity retaining the economic mobility he came for.

We talked with another fellow from El Salvador who had been conscripted into the army as a teen and been forced to kill, which had been a truly hellish time for him. After escaping to the United States, he built a successful home alarm business, making a six-figure income and employing a small team. The recession had cost him his business and his home but not his pride. He was one of the first in the Occupy LA encampment and had become a source of support for others; his tent even had a small solar panel for generating electricity, which he would share when others needed to recharge their batteries.

With each Occupy resident we met, the walls of separation would come down, dissolving the distance that I subtly felt between myself and the Occupiers. Throughout our brief time in the camp, we were treated with open arms. We marveled at the ingenious ways in which the encampment had rallied to provide basics of infrastructure, communication, and governance. Some of the leaders had a wonderful spirit of oneness, even with the police, who were planning to evict them all in a few days. One group offered healing services. Others had created Native American altars. There were moments of poignant solidarity.

On the flip side, we witnessed a fair amount of drunken disorderliness as some turned the encampment into a party. Trash was everywhere. Some people were clearly mentally ill and in real need of help. Some were fresh out of jail and more eager to pick a fight with the police. Others were clearly there out of boredom. There was a shadow side of aimless rebellion for its own sake rather than the focused, disciplined, nonviolent resistance that leaders like Gandhi taught.

After spending about twenty-four hours in the encampment, finding points of real connection with the protestors while also feeling sobered by the suffering, we drove back up the coast toward the San Francisco Bay Area and intentionally stayed in a sumptuous bed and breakfast with a hot tub in the room overlooking the Pacific and wine and cheese in the afternoon. It was an evening of living as the 1 percent, embracing the beauty such a lifestyle can provide. We had moments of guilt and real empathy as we thought of those in the encampment who faced an impending eviction from the police with nowhere to go. The injustice in the situation was clearly apparent. But the truth is that those at the inn who were in a 1 percent lifestyle mode were also decent and kind, perhaps just enjoying a romantic getaway. They might be building businesses that employ people or leading nonprofits that produce real change and just wanting to explore the grace, beauty, and grandeur of the coast. They were not the enemy.

The point for us was not to get too cozy in either identity but to embrace the full spectrum and take seriously the truths held on all sides. We went from sleeping on the hard ground one night, with earplugs to block the noise of passing buses, to staying in an oasis of elegance. If we allow ourselves to get too comfortable in the upscale lifestyle, we can become dissociated from the very real suffering of those who have been marginalized and lose touch with how to help in constructive ways. And if we allow ourselves only to see ourselves as the protestors of an unjust system, an essential truth is also lost—that there is much value in what capitalism has produced.

I share this story to recognize that it's vital for all of us to not become too "occupied" with any one identity. If circumstances were only slightly different we could be on the other end of many things we judge. If I grew up in a slum, I doubt whether I could be where I am today. If I grew up the child of wealth, I might not ever be able to understand what it's like not to have rent money. As someone who has been given a great deal of opportunity, I feel very motivated to give back and to help our systems evolve in a more balanced, just, and compassionate way. The Occupy protestors illuminated some important truths about a system that has come off its moorings and needs deep shifts to realign itself to the noble values that can help us uplevel the American Dream and political operating system.

However, even while appreciating that our system does need to evolve, it doesn't help to judge, hate, or condemn wealthy people, for they are the ones who are often most pivotal in shifting those systems. A handful of awake and engaged billionaires can do remarkable good, and we never know what the next generation will bring. In December 2015, Mark Zuckerberg announced that he would give 99 percent of his stock in Facebook—currently valued at about $45 billion—to philanthropy for the greater good. We recently met with the founders of Nexus, an innovative nonprofit that supports the children of great wealth to become major philanthropic leaders. It is so heartening to hear about what these children of billionaires are committed to creating. If we create a wall in our hearts and leave "them" on the other side of a divide, they no longer feel respected and are prone to retreat into protected enclaves rather than step into their greatest selves in service to the world.

So let us each try to see ourselves in the other and in that way occupy the 100 percent, beginning in our hearts and making it real with our actions. That is how we can put oneness, love, and justice into action. That's how we make things real.

What class of society are we afraid to occupy? Whom do we blame for problems? When we begin to overidentify with being either the 99 percent *or* the 1 percent, that is when we slide into forgetting the truth that we all incarnate here as part of the same team. We are all needed to regrow our nation from the grassroots up—from the Zuccotti Park protestor to the hedge-fund billionaire.

Any movement that leads us to close our heart against another cannot reunite the human family. We might "fix" one problem only to exaggerate the still deeper one. It is time for the divisions to come down. When we can experience ourselves as one people, we will naturally shift our economic system to allow for more opportunity, our political system to ensure greater justice, and our education system to allow greater access to the knowledge needed to thrive.

We all benefit from creating a healthier society that truly works for all, which is really at the heart of America 7.0.

PART THREE

Creating Innovative Solutions

In Part Three, we'll shift our focus to specific solutions that go beyond partisan platforms and that can help America fulfill its mission. Some of these policies and proposals are well developed; some are in the incubation stage; still others are sketches of ideas. All of them, though, offer the possibility of helping to fulfill the sacred potential of our country and our world.

The chapters are not meant to be comprehensive but rather to offer snapshot pictures of how we can approach policies and solutions in a sacred, transpartisan way and help the most promising ones to scale to national or global levels. Some of these policies also aim to create long-term infrastructure that can support ongoing innovation that can move us step by step toward a better future. While we cannot each be involved in all these initiatives, I lay them out here to give hope that effective (and even profitable) solutions are possible in each sector of society.

Building Stronger Families

The family is one of nature's masterpieces.
—George Santayana

I WILL BEGIN PART THREE close to home by focusing on a primary concern for people on the right that tends to be neglected by the left: the creation of strong families. One of the most important critiques from conservatives regarding the cultural shifts of the last decades is that they have led to the deterioration of the nuclear family as the bedrock upon which our society is built. With high (but declining) divorce rates,[1] 22 percent of children living in poverty,[2] and just over 40 percent of kids born out of wedlock,[3] it's right to be distraught that we are not sufficiently investing in creating strong and resilient families that are anchored by solid marriages. Nonetheless, there are also signs of hope, as the rates of teen pregnancy have gone steadily downward in the last twenty years, from 61.8 births per 100,000 in 1991 to 26.5 in 2013 for 15–19-year-olds,[4] and divorce rates have stabilized and even improved.[5]

I believe that we're in a transitional phase as a society and that we need to look with fresh eyes at how to create happy, healthy, and successful families as the bedrock of our society. In our media age, Americans are bombarded with messages every day that can undermine the creation of stable families. There's constant media and Internet distraction, which can prevent us from putting in the time to create loving bonds. There's poor modeling of healthy relationships in TV programs and movies. There's a cultural fascination with doing what makes us feel good in the short term, which can undermine the patience and discipline needed for a long-term marriage. We have high rates of single parenting, a merry-go-round of marriage and divorce, and excessive pornography. Conservatives are right that the traditional nuclear family has never been in as much jeopardy as it is today. And they are also right to point out that divorced families pay a real price in well-being, success, and happiness. Children of divorce fare worse than their peers on many measures, from relational problems to aggression to dropping out of high school.[6] It is therefore in America's best interest to create stronger and more resilient families, which also means stronger and more resilient marriages.

Even fifty years ago, people got very compelling messages, typically from their religious communities, that ensured most people were motivated to take on the long-term discipline and sacrifice a family requires. There was also more fear of social disapproval that kept people from divorcing, as well as less opportunity for single women to stand on their own economically. We certainly don't want to turn back the hands of time on the gains that women have made, but we do need to recognize that we've shifted from a time in which many factors (moral, social, and economic) forced people to stay in families even when they were dysfunctional to an era in which we have to learn how to create healthy, stable families by choice.

In writing this, I don't want to diminish the fact that single parents can and do create happy and healthy families with well-adjusted kids. It's just that when we look at the statistics overall for children of divorce, from doubled rates of suicide to lower graduation rates to being three times as likely to see a psychologist,[7] we're better off as a society with more families anchored by two parents in a long-term loving relationship. And that applies not only to the children but to the parents as well, since married people live longer, happier, and healthier lives, with greater economic security. Divorces lead to more dependency on government assistance, more psychological and economic challenges, and overall less happiness.[8] In short, divorce is costly and damaging for all parties, and it is often taxpayers who pick up part of the tab.

We can no longer impose the conditions for strong families the way social taboos once did. We must therefore focus on education, training, technology, and perhaps even some financial incentives. We'll need to take seriously the science and practice of what helps humans succeed in intimate relationships and navigate challenging times. It's about how we empower more of our citizens with the concrete relational skills necessary for deep partnership and a securely bonded family.

For us to support more resilient families, what is most needed is training from a young age in social and emotional intelligence—the soft skills that allow us to develop and sustain healthy relationships. Many remarkable new programs have been developed that teach children how to communicate their feelings in constructive ways as well as navigate conflicts that arise. One training program, called TOOLBOX by Dovetail Learning, is getting some remarkable results and has ambitions to scale nationally.[9] Building upon more than a decade of development, this program takes some of the core skills of social and emotional intelligence and brings them down to a kid's level of development. The videos of the end result are remarkable: kids who are five or six years old are articulating how they've learned to navigate conflict using terms like "going to a safe place inside" and "talking heart to heart."

Our schools have traditionally focused on mental development and academic subjects like reading and math. But the truth is that emotional and social skills will likely have a greater impact on a child's future success, not only in the workplace but also in future relationships and family life. Another example of innovation is the Quantum Learning Network, which aims to instill eight keys for excellence in kids through SuperCamps and in-school learning programs that build internal capacities for excellence in all situations. They are on their way to their goal of changing the lives of fifty million children.[10] On still another front, Representative Tim Ryan of Ohio has led the way politically in championing the teaching of mindfulness practices within schools as a simple strategy to improve physical health, psychological well-being, social skills, and academic performance. This builds upon the success that mindfulness has shown in realms from the NBA, where the legendary coach Phil Jackson had his players learn it, to Super Bowl champions the Seattle Seahawks. The basic principle is that by developing the internal skill of mindfulness, we can decrease stress, increase emotional resilience, and improve performance through skills like learning how to pay attention.[11]

The work of the nonprofit PassageWorks Institute is also notable in this field, bringing a multidimensional approach to teaching and learning into schools, based on the founder Rachael Kessler's seminal book *The Soul of Education*, which was vetted to appeal to both conservatives and liberals.[12] And one of my favorite nonprofits, Challenge Day, does one-day interventions around the nation that help dissolve cultures of bullying and social isolation that cause so much pain.[13]

Suffice it to say that there are dozens of inspiring initiatives with a common thread of focusing more on the "soft" skills that give kids the internal psychological and relational skills needed to thrive, which have historically not been prioritized in school. Some of these capacities can be built through awareness disciplines like mindfulness, some through enhanced skills to handle anger and other charged emotional states, and still others involve the understanding of what it requires to really build and sustain healthy relationships. By building more of this work into the early stages of development, the skills become more automatic and we harvest the benefits many years later in the form of healthier marriages and families. It's a long-term investment that pays off.

Another key ingredient in strengthening America's families might prove a bit controversial. I think it is essential that we look seriously at providing basic marriage training for anyone who applies for a legal license to marry. Marriage confers many benefits socially and economically, and when a marriage fails there is a large societal cost, especially when there are children involved. Some sources estimate the cost as high as $25,000 per divorce.[14] In order to operate a car legally, we have to understand the basics of how to drive and pass an actual test that confirms we have learned how to be safe. Given the power of a marriage to create issues in our society when it goes awry, why not create national training programs that people can do over the web or on mobile devices, in multiple languages? These programs would train people in principles of communication, navigating conflicts, handling challenging conversations and situations, working out financial issues, and resolving differences—basically giving those who aspire to be legally married in the eyes of the state the latest research into what helps relationships survive and thrive. There could even be secular and specific religious trainings that use language that is more appropriate to someone's belief system. Even better, we might fund national hotlines with trained practitioners to mediate difficult marital situations—a better investment than picking up the pieces after an ugly divorce.

Over the last hundred years of psychotherapy and counseling work, we have learned a great deal about what works and what doesn't to protect and support the bond of a marriage. Much of this is available in books or through high-priced personal therapy, but why not have a national project to integrate the best insights and teachings into multimedia modules that teach the foundational elements of what makes a marriage last—just as a public service?

Creating such a multimedia training, which we might call the Healthy Marriage program, would, on the larger scale of things, require a very small investment in the research and production and, with respected actors playing roles, be compelling and even enjoyable to watch. By enacting specific scenes that show what doesn't work—and what does—we could generate more emotional and relational literacy before people enter marriage or before they hit challenges. A four-to six-hour investment of people's time could pay real dividends down the line when they hit the kind of destructive cycles that are otherwise almost inevitable.

If we're wary of making this kind of training fully mandatory, we could roll it out based on incentives rather than imposition in the following way: when a couple applies for a marriage license, they pay an application fee, which is waived when they demonstrate that they have completed an online program and satisfactorily passed a test about what they've learned. In this way, we'd be providing a financial incentive for people to become more knowledgeable about what it takes to make a marriage work. A more substantial incentive could involve making the ability to file taxes jointly to be predicated on completing the Healthy Marriage program. Given the costs of a failed marriage to society, I think it is wise to financially incentivize something that can increase the odds of success.

This same principle can apply to the core skills of parenting, which could be taught in high school as well as later through technology-assisted means. What if, for example, the American government were to create a program that provides free education based on the latest research on the most effective ways to raise children and navigate the challenges that arise? People might do lessons in ten-minute daily segments—something they can easily listen to in the car or on the train. To increase the motivation to participate, we might make certain things like tax deductions for dependents be contingent on an initial completion of a parenting module, or we could simply allow a larger deduction for those who are current on their parenting training for their children's age.

While the idea of strongly incentivizing education on social and emotional skills for relationships, marriages, and raising kids may at first trigger some resistance, we already have educational requirements to become a driver and the consequences are far more dire from parenting gone awry. Given the massive downstream costs of failure, some small investments up front would pay dividends not only in terms of lowered costs of government assistance but also in terms of building a healthy society.

Educating Our Children

*Grown men may learn from very little children, for the hearts of little
children are pure, and, therefore, the Great Spirit may show to them
many things which older people miss.*
—Black Elk

OUR CHILDREN ARE QUITE literally our future. How we treat
them determines the kind of future we are shaping for America. If
we neglect or abuse them, we sow the seeds of a troubled future. If
we deeply support and lovingly educate our children, we harvest a
harmonious future.

This principle applies not only to our own children. Our
future is created by *all* our children, and thus, if we focus only on
loving, supporting, and nurturing our own children, the rest of the
country may still spiral downward, taking our kids with it. We thus
need to design the next level of American society in such a way
that ultimately leaves no child neglected. That's not just a stance
of compassion. It's a stance that recognizes that we are fundamentally interconnected and that the suffering of one child will, in
some way, affect the happiness and fulfillment of others. We all
pay a cost when a child's formative years go badly.

Whatever role we hold as adults, when we look into the eyes of
an innocent child, we cannot help but be moved to protect them.

A sacred America is a safe America—a place in which children can play and grow and thrive with the full knowledge that the adults in charge are doing their best to create a supportive world for them. Rather than fearing for their survival, children can focus on creativity, learning, and adventure. Bold, curious, and self-confident children are foundational for creating a country and world that truly thrives.

As someone who still hopes to become a parent, I recognize how important raising children is for our growth. The task of tending to a child who is helpless, dependent, and trusting cannot help but make me a more generous, gentle, and loving man. I thus am excited to enter this new phase, even while I recognize the considerable challenges that the role will bring—late nights, diapers, stress, and considerably less free time.

I thus want to honor the role of our children in creating our future and suggest that we build our future first by building it for them. A sacred America can grow only from children who are honored, educated, and empowered in their own uniqueness. Each and every child who is raised with real respect and love will, in turn, be far more likely to create a world that is peaceful, sustainable, healthy, and prosperous. Old cultural habits of polarization and demonization will dissolve through the connective joy of children who learn to live with camaraderie and collaboration.

This perspective leads us to put a very strong emphasis on our schools, which are quite literally the laboratory in which we create our future. When children enter into a world of conflict in schools, they tend to recreate that same world as adults; it becomes their view of what "reality" is like. When they experience schools as a place for adventure, learning, generosity, creativity, and love, they are far more likely to create that world as adults.

Amazing pioneers are working in our schools to create an evolution to a better model of education, some of whom I highlighted in the last chapter on families. One of my favorite organizations,

Challenge Day, was born in 1987 out of one couple's passionate conviction after experiencing some very hard times in junior and high school. Yvonne St. John-Dutra and Rich Dutra-St. John have grown Challenge Day into perhaps the most powerful one-day school intervention ever created, with an extraordinary group of facilitators who travel the full breadth of the United States to help schools make a shift toward a culture based in safety, love, and mutual respect. Former gangbangers, druggies, dropouts, and just plain unhappy students have been transformed into openhearted Challenge Day facilitators who take students on a daylong journey of breaking down walls, cliques, and hatreds to find their shared humanity and connect with their deepest truth. The results have been so powerful that Oprah has done several shows on Challenge Day and worked with them on the creation of a movement.

Imagine if there were Challenge Day facilitators who came to *every* school in our country every year, helping create a shift toward schools in which every child feels safe, loved, and supported. As kids reduced the social fears that feed cycles of isolation and violence, they would more deeply appreciate school and have their attention freed for learning and growth. The impact on our future would be enormous.

Challenge Day is not the only group doing this kind of work, but the breakthroughs are particularly stunning when the walls come down, tough guys confess their wounds, bullies apologize for their bullying, and youths on the verge of suicide find friends and allies. If we can eliminate the culture of social isolation, fear, and loneliness, students can learn far better and, perhaps more importantly, have a model for the kind of culture they will create as adults. If we minimize or eliminate violence, bullying, and teasing in our schools, kids will grow up more resilient, self-confident, and creative.

Our schools should really, then, be our unifying focus as a country. Our schools are where we build America's future, person by person. When kids emerge scarred, fearful, broken, violent, or alone, we have set them up for a damaged adulthood.

Schools have also been one of the biggest battlegrounds politically, as the value systems of Democrats, Republicans, and Independents often don't align on how or what to teach. One of the most exciting developments to break this gridlock comes from a recent two-year collaboration orchestrated and led by the Convergence Center for Policy Resolution, an innovative nonprofit that aims to create cohesive, grounded, and effective policies through transpartisan collaborations and working groups. To help reimagine education from the ground up, they convened a working group with twenty-six high-level representatives that represented a full spectrum of political persuasions, from progressive to Libertarian. While it wasn't always easy, they eventually came together on a report called "Education Reimagined: A Transformational Vision for Education in the US"[1] that has won kudos from across the political spectrum and puts the learner at the center of education. This is exactly the kind of initiative that can open us up to a whole new era of education for our kids.[2]

An additional strategy for a transformation of American schools would be to work with more experimental schools in which the best programs, trainings, and tools available are brought to bear on creating a learning environment that delivers tools for emotional development, personal empowerment, and skills beyond learning information, in addition to the best accelerated learning programs. If we did our best to create top-notch templates that harness all our best-in-class tools for growth and personal transformation in addition to the skills required for individual excellence, we would have powerful laboratories in which to design the future of education. The task for our state governments would then be to take the best models from the leading-edge schools and rapidly replicate the most effective programs.

For too long, the technologies of personal growth have only been applied to adults. It is time that we translate these practices and techniques into forms that kids in schools can use. Why shouldn't our children learn skills of emotional intelligence, stress reduction, or life coaching from a young age? Our schools can become far better incubators of a sacred future for America if we are willing to see them as the most important place to apply our newest innovations, highest ideals, and best technologies for growth. And that, in turn, can create a new generation of education for conscious, secure, creative, and engaged Americans.

Creating a Culture of Peace

Blessed are the peacemakers, for they
shall be called the children of God.
—Matthew 5:9

IN THIS CHAPTER, WE will begin to explore some of the more challenging areas for public policy and show how we can approach these
issues in novel ways that build from a sacred worldview and integrate the values of both left and right. The next chapters will particularly focus on issues of peace and security and how left and right
can work together to create a safe America and a peaceful world.
We'll go from templating a culture of peace locally to looking at
how the United States can create stability in the Middle East.

Everywhere we turn, it seems, we are surrounded by violence.
War, murder, crime, child abuse, domestic abuse, and violent
sports: they are all woven into the fabric of our world—and especially American culture.

We have just emerged from the bloodiest century in recorded
history only to start our new millennium with conflagrations
around the globe and the "war without end" on terrorism, including the latest horrors of ISIS.

While it is easy to be dismayed by violence elsewhere, in
many ways America is a leading perpetrator. We are the biggest

manufacturer and seller of arms, selling 30 percent of all the weapons in the world.[1] Our homicide rates have been the worst in Western developed countries for sixty years,[2] and our incarceration rates are the highest in the world, at 716 per 100,000 as of October 2013.[3] And our entertainment offers a continual stream of violence for an eager global audience.

What will it take to shift our culture away from one founded on violence to one in which our bedrock principles are based on peace? That question has provoked many great thinkers, activists, and change agents. We'll explore one such pathway in this chapter.

It begins with the recognition that if our task is to create a shift to a culture of peace on a national and global scale, we need to be able to demonstrate how that is possible on a local scale. Through a powerful demonstration project that harnesses best practices, pioneering programs, and social innovations, we can show that a shift from a culture of violence to a culture of peace is possible. Once such a demonstration project is successful on a local level, the teachings, infrastructure, practices, and collaborations that work can be brought into new areas. In many ways, this represents the same approach as most startup components: build a proof of concept, get it working well, then scale it and replicate it in new markets. Working with a smaller size initially allows us to test approaches more easily with fewer resources.

Creating a local demonstration project for shifting to a culture of peace is part of the idea behind the Summer of Peace, which we began at The Shift Network with a yearly program of three-month virtual online conferences that bring many of the most significant peacebuilders and organizations into synergistic relationship with each other. It is now the largest online peace event each year, featuring hundreds of the top pioneers, all of which ends up in a free World Peace Library. As our Director of Peace Philip Hellmich likes to say, this cross-sector approach is leading to a new narrative of peace from inner to international. By bridging many different perspectives, from mediators to military experts and scientists to spiritual teachers, we are beginning to see the patterns that connect them all into a holistic approach to peace and security.

This online resource library with the world's top peacebuilders can then inform a local-level demonstration project. By weaving together best practices from dozens of nonprofit groups, marshaling the best science on practices of peace, enrolling citizens in participatory processes at a neighborhood level, and encouraging personal peace pledges through events and web media, we believe that it is possible to demonstrate a dramatic long-term reduction in the baseline of crime and violence in a single city, which can then be studied and replicated.

This goal will be challenging, and it will require massive participation as well as synchronization between efforts in education, criminal justice, policing, and social services. It will require spiritual practices, communication training, and efforts to heal community trauma. And it will require a shift toward restorative justice, community policing, and innovative programs to work with violent offenders. In short, it will require a collaboration between both engaged citizens and government officials, working from the level of law, courts, police, and criminal justice to neighborhood interventions with troubled youth and gangs.

The number of elements required to shift to a culture of peace is long, but virtually every step has noble-minded groups, dedicated individuals, and well-developed programs addressing the need. For example, Aqeela Sherrills is a renowned peacemaker from Watts who helped broker the ceasefire between two rival LA gangs, the Crips and the Bloods, in 1992. That ceasefire is credited with creating a dramatic drop in violence in the area. He developed the Community Passage to Peace Initiative (CPP) with the Unity One Foundation to address the state of youth gang relations in strategic communities and to catalyze a movement for peace in urban communities across the country. The goal of the CPP is to create a national model for how peace is created and sustained in urban war zones, turning it into a movement for social change and prosperity in our communities.

Their approach focuses on the root cause of problems that face young people, coupled with hiring community leaders who have long-term relationships with the communities they serve. Aqeela's program is sophisticated, powerful, and integrated. It includes the need for community grieving and healing, mentoring, use of the arts, and more. And it is born from facing the worst suffering head-on: Aqeela lost thirteen friends and his own son Terrell to gang violence. Instead of retaliating with violence for this killing, Aqeela turned his son's death into a call for compassion, understanding, and peacebuilding.

In each sector of society, there are remarkable programs like Aqeela's that are emerging, often led by the people who were once on the front lines of violence. Most, though, are underfunded and not adequately visible. And there is neither adequate coordination among the programs nor a systematic way for the rest of the society to become part of the solution.

Our Summer of Peace vision is to create an experimental platform to address this need—to weave together many effective programs and make them more impactful and visible, as well as enroll citizens to be part of the solution themselves. The most likely first location to ground this vision is Oakland, California, a place undergoing much creative change and evolution that also has a history of violence. This city would become our pilot project for demonstrating what is possible with a truly comprehensive approach. Interestingly enough, when we started moving this work forward, we discovered that there were already two other cities, Milwaukee and Philadelphia, with their own Summer of Peace initiatives that are moving in this direction. I always take that as a positive sign when the same idea emerges in parallel.

Once we are able to make a stronger local demonstration of a real cultural shift, our vision is that the Summer of Peace will move to other cities and countries to replicate successes, incorporate new programs and ideas, and foster best practices for creating a cultural shift to peace. It would leave behind a Department of Peace in each city that coordinates and supports the programs that worked and communicates with other cities that are experimenting with such a whole-systems approach as well. With each successive summer, there will be a growing sophistication about which programs are most effective. A scientific team could help advance the scientific study while a consultative group will advise governments about how to implement some of the best programs long term.

As part of building toward this vision, we've activated a Peace Ambassador Training that has trained over a thousand peace ambassadors around the world, with a special focus on Oakland and Detroit in America. Former director of Amnesty International in Washington, DC, James O'Dea designed the initial curriculum and has detailed his practical, scientific, and spiritual synthesis to peacebuilding in his book *Cultivating Peace*, which is highly recommended. It has since evolved under the leadership of Philip Hellmich and Emily Hine to a 2.0 version that incorporates the work on the science of mindfulness and compassion.

The work of building a culture of peace has a long history, with millions working tirelessly on all the key elements. Peacebuilding was a foundational motive for the very creation of the United Nations, as well as numerous UN treaties. Breaking humanity's addiction to violence as a means to resolve conflict has not been an easy process. However, I think it is now time for this work to go to the next level of sophistication. Creating a culture of peace is not just about fixing wars between nation-states but about building the principles and practices of peace into the foundation of our families, schools, and communities.

In this way, a successful, locally templated Summer of Peace can demonstrate how we can shift to a culture of peace in one place by combining best-in-class innovations and thus lay the groundwork for the eventual creation of a truly peaceful America and a planetary culture of peace.

16

Beyond a War on Terror

There never was a good war or a bad peace.
—Benjamin Franklin

WHILE WE ARE DISCUSSING America becoming a leader in peace innovation, I want to shift our focus to the national level and the articulation of a peaceful mission around which we can orient that aligns our country with the upgrade to America 7.0.

Our president typically defines our national mission either explicitly or implicitly. That mission provides the primary direction for us to move as a people. Clarifying and articulating a sense of direction is one of the main roles for political leaders. Jim Collins's management book *Good to Great* emphasizes the importance of a tenacious, hedgehog-like dedication to a singular focus as the key to creating a profitable and enduring company. The same is true of sports teams, political campaigns, and churches. Finding and articulating a Big Dream that can inspire people to move in the same direction is at the core of effective leadership.

Our country has more than 320 million citizens,[1] and aligning a majority of those citizens in the same direction is no small task. But without that alignment, our potential as a country is lost in the swirl of personal agendas and political infighting. We operate with mediocrity, too much of our creative energy dissipated on competing concerns.

So America, like any large group, needs a shared focus to activate our highest potential. What mission can galvanize our greatness, inspire our service, and help us to create something of enduring value? What is today's equivalent of a lunar landing, the goal that can unify a nation and inspire people to "ask not what your country can do for you, ask what you can do for your country"?

After 9/11, President Bush articulated the war on terror as our shared focus. It was the political drumbeat of his administration, and we spent considerable money and time honing our skill at fighting that war, which then led us into invasions of Afghanistan and Iraq, both of which were expensive and damaging in the long term. The Obama administration never articulated as clear a focus for its own Big Mission, so to some extent we have reduced the ambitions and scale of the war on terror without ever dismantling that as our core American mission.

A war can sometimes be effective for temporarily galvanizing and focusing a country. Stopping Hitler in World War II was a noble cause. That war inspired great sacrifice for the good of the whole. After 9/11, the war on terror gave our country something to rally around and provided a collective focus for our pain and outrage. In its beneficial aspects, it inspired sacrifice for the good of the collective.

However, using war as America's long-term orienting mission generates many problems in addition to the legacy of destruction and loss of life, which is already a very steep price to pay. Wars are, at their very best, short-term solutions to complex situations. With winning a war as our mission, our drive toward excellence becomes focused at honing our war-making prowess. Success becomes measured by our military dominance in battle, which is ultimately destructive, rather than our success in culture building, which is far more constructive. In the heat of preparing for battle, we forget that the actual desired outcome, even for most hawks, is peace. War is only a means to reach that end.

John F. Kennedy chose putting a man on the moon as the audacious collective mission of his day that could inspire America's national focus. Lyndon Johnson's Great Society legislation carried a similar big dream. Martin Luther King Jr.'s Beloved Community also carried a magnetic appeal of a high-minded and worthy goal that could unify us. Ronald Reagan inspired America with his vision of a Shining City on a Hill. The problem with using a war as our orienting focus is that it trains our vision on a problem, polarizes around the "source" of that problem, and tends to focus on short-term destruction of the perceived source of the problem rather than long-term building of our culture.

It thus tends to be revolutionary and impulsive versus evolutionary and long term. When our articulated mission is all about defeating an enemy, there is not a productive set of measures and goals for the vast majority of society to benchmark against. After all, if I am not toting a gun in Afghanistan, how am I contributing to succeeding in the war on terror? It is not sufficiently inclusive nor is it inspiring enough to bring all of us into long-term support.

When we focus America's collective intention on the means (a war on terror) rather than the end (a world at peace), a number of things also happen. First, we create unnecessary polarities between hawks and doves. When America's shared public mission is the war on terror, there's not a real role for peacemakers and pacifists, who represent an important part of our population, and they end up being viewed just in opposition. However, if we shift our focus to a higher objective, where we're focused on creating a world at peace, the skills of the peacemaker *and* the military leader are both required in different situations. As an orienting compass, then, a war on terror fails to include both polarities while exaggerating power struggles between them. The mission of creating a world at peace includes both political polarities and all of our citizens.

In addition, the war on terror as a mission skews us heavily toward imbalanced masculine modes of governance. Power moves toward those who are most adept at conducting a war, typically men. As a country, we move away from masculine-feminine balance, which undermines our ability to create wholeness in our culture.

Using the war on terror as a collective mission also fails to instill a vision of a positive outcome that can inspire people for long-term service and sacrifice. When our intention is focused on war, we tend to increase the psychology of fear that fuels and perpetuates war (and in the end fuels terrorism). We create a martial climate. The power of our subconscious is harnessed to create the conditions for more war rather than accelerate the building of peace.

Using the war on terror as our long-term mission also undermines the trust of other nations. They begin to see us as committed to military dominance rather than peacemaking prowess. A world at peace can be a unifying mission for all countries, but a war on terror tends to pit different nations or blocs of nations against each other.

Finally, putting our focus on war can lead to a sense of hopelessness, depression, and fear. The often gloomy atmosphere of America in our first decade of the new millennium was partially a reflection of a life-negating mission at the forefront of our consciousness for too long. Even the mission of restoring America's economy tends not to be aspirational enough, as it's essentially about our self-interest rather than our service. Without a positive, inspiring sense of mission, we begin to feel less proud and more cynical, which has debilitating effects on our national psychology.

Shifting our collective intention to focus on a broader and more inspiring mission of a world at peace—rather than one strategy to achieve that goal (the war on terror)—holds the potential of bringing people together from across the political spectrum as we recognize that we all hold complementary pieces of achieving the collective mission. When we commit our country at the most fundamental level to excellence at peacemaking, we can reconnect with a more positive view of ourselves and find allies at home and abroad. That doesn't mean we dismantle our defenses or immediately defund the military. They just become part of working together toward a higher and more unifying cause.

While Obama did commit to winding down two major war theaters, he never did articulate a grand, overarching cause for the United States to replace the war on terror. Instead, he positioned himself as a more modest and strategic general than Bush in the war on terror without fundamentally redefining our country's mission. If he or a subsequent president were able to instead focus America's intention on the higher goal of creating a world at peace (or a still more comprehensive mission), it would begin to unite us again even while there may be short-term military actions required.

Long term, it is vital that enlightened political leadership puts America's focus on the highest, most inclusive, forward-looking mission, such as creating a world at peace, with any wars seen as a method of last resort. An aspirational public mission, calling upon us to transcend our limitations in the service of a noble cause, would, like landing a man on the moon, unleash far more creative energy and passion.

17

Consecrating the Warrior

Do I not destroy my enemies when I make them my friends?
—Abraham Lincoln

IN SHIFTING TOWARD AN orientation of creating a world at peace, one of the most challenging questions then becomes, How do we handle the warrior qualities and capacities that we've developed in our country? This is true not just at the level of political leadership but at all levels of our country.

As we've discussed, we are a country steeped in violence, from our high abuse and murder rates to our enjoyment of blood sports like UFC to our excitement at crushing the "enemy" in battle. Like the Romans who encouraged and cultivated martial culture through coliseum "sport" and battlefield glory, Americans have been trained to love violence in film, games, and sport, which has fed into our growth as earth's dominant military power.

Many peaceworkers believe that we will simply outgrow our martial tendencies and that we will no longer be so aggressive once we evolve to the next level as a country. Peace, in their view, becomes a transcendence of the more primitive qualities that now often dictate human behavior. We are imagined to evolve into an idyllic condition in which we all get along.

I believe that our evolutionary path forward requires something different. Once a capacity is built, it is human nature not to want to lose it. Right-wing fears of giving more power to the United Nations reflect this desire to retain the power, strength, and dominance we've achieved rather than cede it. America's resistance to some international accords also relates to fear of loss of power. Even if rational analysis reveals that global agreements hold greater promise to solve problems such as war and global warming, emotionally it is hard for some Americans to relinquish the power that we've amassed.

The left tends to dislike the mentality behind martial dominance. The right tends to celebrate it. Neither side is providing a true path forward for how the virtues that are foundational to martial excellence can be harnessed in the service of the evolution of all humanity. I say virtues because the disciplines required to become a strong warrior are not easy to master. To become physically, emotionally, and mentally strong requires a disciplined practice of going beyond limitations. America is a young nation, and to rise to global military dominance so quickly has required remarkable excellence from our military as well as from the economic, scientific, and technological engine behind the scenes. Many countries have vied for military dominance at some point in history, and the fact that we've achieved it is a mark of excellence.

That said, now that we've become "number one," what do we do with that warrior power? Empires can and do become stagnant and self-indulgent, like a professional athlete who retires and becomes a couch potato. Is that America's fate? How will we find better uses for our accumulated military prowess and all the skills we've developed to produce that?

I see two main things that need to happen for America's warrior qualities to be consecrated in the service of the next stage of evolution. The left needs to embrace more of the virtues and disciplines that create warrior strength. They need to see the fire of sports, the driven intensity of business, and a strong and effective military as potential engines for the good. The full embrace of warrior disciplines allows more left-wing and spiritually oriented folks to demonstrate the physical, emotional, and mental strength that those on the right require of their leaders, and thus be embraced as political leaders. I see it as a good sign when those on the left are excited by weightlifting or capitalism.

The right needs to outgrow narrowly defined self-interest. When the warrior is dedicated only to the service of narrow interests, he or she becomes more destructive. When warrior virtues are self-centered, the sense of care and compassion for others diminishes. Self-centered warriors become good at amassing power, money, and strength but are increasingly low on ethics and often even abusive with their power.

Those on the left often dissociate from the warrior side, or diminish its value. So they may become less adept at being strong, productive, and self-reliant. They resent the power and money amassed by conservatives and want it to flow more equitably rather than simply compete for those resources in the capitalist game. Their warrior side tends to come out in right-wing critiques, which can be strong on intellectual logic and weaker on personal responsibility.

The way I see it, neither is in right relationship with their warrior side. One identifies with it for personal gain while the other splits from it in a way that abdicates power. The path forward for America, I believe, requires a different relationship with our well-honed warrior qualities, one that truly consecrates them in the service of something higher, like a Renaissance knight who pledges himself to protect and serve a lady, or a police officer who pledges to serve the community.

A truly spiritual warrior consecrates his or her "sword" for the liberation or betterment of all beings. Not just Christians or Americans or Buddhists, Muslims, and Jews. Everyone. Mahatma Gandhi was a spiritual warrior, expressing his warrior qualities in the form of intense personal disciplines and strong social action. He and his followers acted for the liberation of India and the transformation of the British Empire. In World War II, Americans summoned the warrior side of our nation to halt Hitler's march and Japan's aggression, a noble service for the entire world.

Because we are the most powerful nation on earth militarily, it is essential for us to evolve our martial excellence into something that truly serves the good of the whole planet. That would mean that we are putting our military forward truly in service to all, from halting wars to intervening in the rebuilding of countries. Instead of using our military as an instrument of empire building to benefit ourselves economically, we'd truly be pledging these skills and trainings to the greater good of the planet.

Such a consecration, though, is likely to happen only when a critical mass of American citizens evolve a different relationship with their own warrior side, taking the middle path forward of embracing the warrior qualities and virtues while using them in service to all beings.

This path is ultimately a path of love, which integrates all aspects of our nature and offers them up in a spirit of generosity. Such a path reduces violence rather than reveling in it. When America's martial dominance and warrior virtues can be offered up in service to Israelis *and* Palestinians, Americans *and* Iranians, then we will begin to create a world that is truly at peace.

Part of this consecration will also require men to be initiated into a more mature version of the warrior and ultimately manhood. In traditional cultures the world over from African to Native American, it was almost universally believed that boys needed to face an initiatory ordeal in order to enter manhood. They needed to face their inner dragon, tame their fears, transcend their selfish impulses, and be blessed by elder men into their full power. Initiation turned boys into men and rebellious youths into wise leaders.

The process was not instantaneous, but the initiatory ordeal was key to disciplining the warrior forces in a boy and shaping them into mature manhood. In today's world, many men's organizations have emerged that are offering a similar rite of passage. Perhaps foremost among these is the ManKind Project, which created the New Warrior Training Adventure—a weekend process that has initiated more than fifty thousand men into a new kind of brotherhood and masculine power. This kind of program needs to become the norm.

Simply dismissing the warrior will do no good; the warrior energy lives too deeply in the male psyche and in our cultural ideals. Warriors know they are here to serve, and it is simply a matter of giving them a high and noble enough way to serve along with the discipline and brotherhood for their natural protective instincts to be aligned with the good of our world. That is what can begin to turn more warriors into wise kings.

A final key ingredient for peace leadership moving forward, one that is essential to cultivate at the same time as the healthy warrior, is an open heart, which generates the compassion and inspiration that true "peace warriors" need. It is not enough for this love to extend to only a few; it needs to spread broadly to encompass the whole of our society and our world. Jesus's saying "love thy neighbor as thyself" serves as kind of a first commandment to evolve this kind of leadership.

Having an open heart is not easy in today's world since we are exposed to a range of tragedy and trauma through media. Our hearts want to recoil from the evening news, with stories of murder, terrorist threats, or economic doom. It can be overwhelming to immerse ourselves in the grief of a Syrian widow, the outrage of a legless Iraqi youth, the pain of a Congolese rape victim, or the desperate hunger of a Sudanese refugee. How much can we open to these situations and retain a positive outlook, one infused with trust and a spirit of possibility?

One of America's gifts to the world is our optimism, but that gift can carry a shadow of indifference to the plight of others, especially those we perceive to be our enemies. Once someone is in the category of "enemy" we convince ourselves of the need to be heartless and brutal, strong-arming the opposition into submission to make us "safe." Perhaps the most unfortunate part is when America's martial attitude is paired with a dedication to Jesus. Jesus's most central teaching was to love the enemy. This teaching is at the sacred core of his work, challenging us to open our hearts so wide that we exclude no one, even those who attack or wrong us. Instead, we are asked to forgive those who wrong us not just seven times but "seventy times seven times."

Who among us has lived this teaching fully? It is certainly not easy—millennia of biological programming drive us toward retaliation violence and revenge when threatened. But with humanity's ever-increasing capacity to destroy, if we let ourselves be driven only by our biological codes, we accelerate the forces that are taking humanity over a cliff. I believe we have to take seriously Jesus's challenge if we want to survive and create a peaceful world. If we cannot find love for those we now see as our enemies, the spiral of retribution and fear continues, preventing us from rising to meet the great challenges of our day. This doesn't preclude military or police action at times—there is a need for protection and defense by the warrior when there are people who seek to harm others. We must honor the need for laws and prevent anarchic behavior that harms others, at both a local level and a global level. Until we can contain rogue states and terrorism, there will be an important role for the military.

However, can we engage the necessary actions without losing the love in our heart? That ensures we don't polarize against a part of our human family and create negative spirals that can endure for generations.

So as we hear of terrorist plots or beheadings by ISIS and witness devastating wars, let us dare to practice what Jesus taught. Instead of feeding the cycle of fear and contraction and discrimination, let us instead encourage a spiral of love, holding all sides in a vision of healing, even while choosing to take those actions that are necessary for safety and protection. It is a practice that may not come naturally. But when we speak, think, and act from an openhearted stance ourselves, we can begin to reverse the contraction of humanity's heart. At an advanced level, we can cultivate the openheartedness and the protective power of a true warrior at the same time. *That* is true spiritual warriorship.

Ultimately, it's what determines whether we will be part of the force that lifts humanity toward peace or whether we will allow fear and separation to seduce us toward our collective demise. We have the opportunity to choose with every breath, every thought, and every deed.

18

Stabilizing the Middle East

I don't think anybody who carries a rifle carries the future. Because I don't believe you can really change the world by killing and shooting. You have to change it by creating and competing.
—Shimon Peres

WHILE IT IS ESSENTIAL to begin at home and address the roots of violence in our own hearts, communities, and culture, it's also important that America support a more sophisticated and effective approach to peacebuilding in the world—particularly in the Middle East, where we've gotten into the most trouble in recent decades. There is no more problematic area for violence, war, and instability right now, and the sheer momentum of problems may propel America still deeper into wars again.

While it is impossible to anticipate the latest developments and the specific challenges under way at the time you read this book, I do want to highlight a set of deeper shifts that can help America contribute to creating peace in the Middle East. These recommendations go beyond the alliances and agreements of today to long-term tectonic shifts in our consciousness, our policies, and our relationship with the many peoples in the region. The United States needs to walk carefully in this arena, for we've made many missteps in the past, partially due to our cultural ignorance and biases in how we engage.

I believe these tectonic shifts will need to happen in a number of areas:

- First, we need to shift from being a primarily military actor to a leading stabilizing force, which means that we strengthen and deepen our relationships in the Middle East broadly rather than choosing sides and funding or leading wars.

- Second, we need to heal our country's relationship with Islam, shifting from a stance of fear, disrespect, and discrimination to one of curiosity, respect, and brother-hood.

- Third, we'll need to develop a relationship with Iran as an ally rather than an enemy and build bridges of cultural and economic exchange with this key regional player.

- Fourth, we'll need to really commit ourselves to the healing of millennia of trauma, including owning up to the parts that we've co-created.

- Fifth, we'll need to support the gradual, long-term evo-lution, education, and development of societies there.

- And sixth, we'll have to help find the way to support the satisfactory resolution of the Palestinian situation.

And we'll have to do all this without undermining our rela-tionship with Israel, which is both a beloved ally with the highest-functioning democracy in the region and sometimes a stumbling block to larger peacekeeper efforts.

These six areas are by no means comprehensive; but I do think the instability and violence that have come to characterize the region can be decreased dramatically as we engage these longer-term shifts in relationship to the Middle East.

The first and most important area is to shift from using our military to force the changes we think are required to primarily building alliances and serving as a stabilizing presence. Almost every time we intervene with either covert or overt military operations, we eventually end up causing a downward spiral for the simple reason that wherever there is more chaos, the more brutal players tend to seize power. ISIS, for example, was directly created out of the power vacuum left when we toppled Saddam Hussein and fired all of his Sunni military leaders, who suddenly were jobless and ripe for enrollment in a destructive cause.

On other fronts, the current antagonism of Iran toward the United States arose partially as a result of our CIA's involvement in the coup that brought Shah Pahlavi to power in 1953 as well as our ongoing support of the shah's rule, which then triggered the Islamic Revolution in 1979 that installed Ayatollah Khomeini. The current ayatollah Ali Khamenei's violent rhetoric against America is undoubtedly colored by his time in a prison under the shah's rule with SAVAK torturers who had reputedly been trained by CIA and Mossad operatives.[1] Elsewhere, Libya's Muammar Gaddafi was a truly terrible ruler, to be sure, but once we helped to topple him, the country descended into greater chaos and suffering.

The basic pattern is that each time America intervenes with our military or CIA, we eventually create breakdowns that shift more power toward increasingly bad actors who create more chaos. This makes sense when we understand what author Don Beck calls Spiral Dynamics—the natural progression of organizational systems in parallel with growth in consciousness. When a certain level of organization is quickly removed, it is very rare to have the next higher level build; instead we tend to see cultural regression to a previous level. That core insight helps us to see why it's far better to work with totalitarian regimes, which have a certain ordering and stabilizing function, than choose to intervene with force. The force will almost always cause cultural regression, often to previous identities such as religious or tribal loyalties.

So basically, a high-level understanding of cultural development shows us that when we rapidly destroy or undermine a fragile structure of governance, it tends to lead to cultural regress rather than progress. Not only that, because we are seen as the largest global military empire and acting mainly in our self-interest, when we do intervene militarily, we generate long-term animosity toward us that acts like a poison beneath the surface.

The principle in medical training to "first, do no harm" is for good reason; a botched intervention can often make things worse than the disease we are trying to cure. If we instead focus on broad alliance building with as many governments as we can, as well as respecting UN resolutions and international law, we are more likely to be perceived as a positive, stabilizing force. At the same time, we can bolster the activities of successful private and NGO initiatives that *are* making a long-term difference in the Middle East. Over time, these more distributed people-to-people initiatives empower more lasting change because they encourage sustainable and balanced development. For a deeper understanding, I recommend reading *Spiral Dynamics* by Don Beck and Christopher Cowan, which has been helpful to me in understanding how to manage and honor the complexity of many worldviews and help them develop over time rather than descend into chaos.[2]

The second major area for reform in our stance in the Middle East is to make it our duty as Americans to truly understand and respect Islam to help dissipate the growing energy of animosity that fuels terrorism and war. When we cannot truly honor a group's religion—which is at the very core of how they make sense of their life and give meaning to their world—we have very shaky ground for further relationship. Gandhi wrote in *Young India* that "if we are to respect others' religions as we would have them respect our own, a friendly study of the world's religion is a sacred duty."

Far too many Americans are challenged to relate respectfully to the Muslim world, an issue that predates 9/11 or ISIS. People from across the political spectrum assume that Islam is a dangerous religion designed to goad its followers into religiously motivated violence rather than champion peace. Reactionaries go so far as to make slurs about the religion as a whole. A 2015 poll found that 55 percent of Americans hold either a somewhat or very unfavorable view of Islam.[3] There is an uneasy feeling that the modern West and Islam are like oil and water, even though we have 2.77 million Muslim Americans who tend to be reasonably prosperous, integrated, and proud to be American.[4] Healing our psychological rift with this global religion of 1.6 billion people may be the single most essential act in stabilizing the Middle East as well as creating a truly peaceful global community. Breaking a negative cycle on either side can lead to an opening of the relationship: change in the other is easier if we first change ourselves. If we first recognize our oneness with Muslims and then find deep respect for the essence of their religion, it becomes possible to engage in much more truthful and loving relationship with them.

Often non-Islamic Westerners will fixate on the parts of Islam that are obviously out of balance—radical jihadists, extreme attitudes toward women, or harsh indictments of Western morals. If we critique those elements from a stance of separateness, without respect for the sacred core of Islamic religion or the Prophet Mohammed, we will tend to put a match to the kindling of festering frustrations.

Whatever someone holds as sacred is at the core of his or her vision for a better world. If we take seriously the need to celebrate the great blessing, illumination, and transformation that Islam has brought to people around the world, we can begin to move back toward respectful relationship with the hearts of Muslim cultures.

And that, in turn, will soften the political divides, culture clashes, and historical animosities, as well as create common ground upon which partnerships can be built.

Ultimately, what we really need is an Abrahamic family reunion—for Christians, Jews, and Muslims to realize that we all share common ancestry. We have put our focus on different holy texts and prophets, but the truth is that we all flow from the same source. The more we can honor our common roots, the less polarized we will be in navigating our differences.

Reconnecting with our Islamic brothers and sisters as part of our extended family will go a long way to creating a world at peace, which is the ultimate goal of the Islamic religion since Islam literally means "peace through submission to God." Such a family reunion cannot happen at gunpoint. It will happen through a spirit of mutual honoring, cultural exchange, American media that explores Islamic life, events that weave the cultures together, and political accords that find common cause in building a peaceful world in which our religious traditions can respectfully coexist.

There are many beautiful groups doing this work of reunifying the Abrahamic family, from the Abrahamic Reunion to interfaith groups in the Parliament of the World's Religions. America can play a leading role in what this looks like—to encourage the family reunion at all levels rather than stoke isolationist fears or outright discrimination.

The third area where I believe America will need to evolve is in our relationship with Iran, a relationship that has been ice-cold since the 1979 revolution and hostages crisis. Even with the 2015 Iran nuclear deal, the relationship remains very polarized. Transforming this relationship is vital because there are two primary ideological divides in the Middle East, and Iran plays a key role in both. The first is the Sunni–Shiite divide, which dates back to the immediate succession claims after the death of the Prophet Mohammed. Many wars are still ultimately sourced in animosity between Sunnis and Shiites. As I write this, there are proxy wars in places like Yemen playing out along Sunni and Shiite lines, which are backed by Saudi Arabia on the Sunni side and Iran on the Shiite side. Both nations are jockeying for regional leadership through these proxy wars, which add fuel to the fire of regional instability.

The other primary divide has been between Islam and the Jewish people. Iran has again played a primary role, taking a strongly anti-Israel stance and supporting groups like Hamas and Hezbollah. Because Iran plays a key role in both of these polarities, when we engage with them as the enemy by completely siding with Israel or Saudi Arabia, we provoke more animosity and escalate tensions. Our goal should be to reduce rather than inflame tensions.

Opening to the possibility of a real détente with Iran and the eventual creation of another ally in the region is essential for long-term peace prospects. That's because Iran is a large country (seventy million people) and a relatively developed one, with sophisticated education and economic systems. It has a great deal of history as an epicenter for Islamic learning, such as in the Golden Age, as well as a history as one of the largest empires of ancient times. Today, a large percentage of its population (about 70 percent) is below the age of thirty, and that younger generation is generally pro-Western and supportive of America, particularly because they track American entertainment and music culture closely.[5]

Modern Iran also has a highly educated population of women, including more than 60 percent of current university students. So while the threats that come from the Ayatollah and the hardline religious leaders who surround him can be extreme (and quite frightening), the truth beneath the surface is that there is a whole new generation that listens to American music and watches American TV programs. They embrace America and are eager to become friends. Iran also has a large diaspora population, including more than one million Iranians in the United States—many of whom have reached a high level of success and can serve as ambassadors.

Once the thaw begins in earnest, which I suspect will start to happen after the sanctions lift in 2016, there can be bridges built between the considerable expatriate community and the next generation within Iran. I expect there will emerge a natural softening of the animosity through exchanges on the cultural and business levels as well. We witnessed a similar process with China where the leadership engaged in gradual cultural shifts toward capitalism and market reforms even while keeping the communist political structure in place. As the cultural thawing begins, it will create the opportunity for a stabilization of the two biggest divides in the Middle East and potentially the defunding of proxy conflicts— especially if we become legitimate allies of all three key regional players: Israel, Saudi Arabia, and Iran.

While Israel and Saudi Arabia might feel resistant to the United States choosing to befriend a current "enemy," the truth is that the best way to stabilize the region is to deepen relationships with all sides and work toward de-escalation and demilitarization, from the nuclear agreement already enacted with Iran to cease-fires in other areas. Those three countries can eventually act as a stabilizing tripod for the whole Middle East if we help to create the base between them.

America does have a history of being able to turn sworn enemies into important allies, which then helps to stabilize an entire region. In World War II, the Germans were the hated enemy of the United States; but we chose to become allies over time and, in turn, Germany has anchored the development of a war-free Europe. Japan was also a sworn enemy that became a close ally and helped to create a more peaceful Pacific Rim. Because of the deep vein of pro-American sentiment in the next generation of Iranians, as well as their long history of cultural and intellectual leadership in that part of the world, Iran has the potential to become the key to stabilizing the Middle East. But we'll need to take the time to see Iran with the eyes of respect and build bridges on many levels.

At The Shift Network, we are in the early stages of planning a Gifts of Iran telesummit to understand more about the history of the country, from the vast ancient Persian empires to the first human-rights declaration to the flowering of scientific wisdom in the Islamic Golden Age to the great mystical inheritance of their poets such as Rumi, Hafez, and Attar. We're also planning to bring a tourism group to the country in late 2016 to build personal bridges, which are essential for mutual understanding.

It can be equally valuable for each of us to simply reach out to Iranians as friends. During one of our events in 2012, for instance, an Israeli named Tal tearfully hugged a woman named Nahid from Iran onstage, declaring that they loved each other and honored each other as brother and sister. It was a truly touching moment as they embraced across the political divides, which brought the audience to tears.

The fourth area to shift in relationship to the Middle East is to bring more expertise and resources into healing the trauma of millennia of violence. So long as the peoples of the region are still traumatized, they will react to current realities based on past stories. Traumatized people are far easier to goad into war or extremist ideologies. The last decades have seen remarkable developments in the healing of trauma, from mindfulness training to EMDR (eye movement desensitization and reprocessing) therapy to social-healing dialogue groups to schools of psychotherapy that focus specifically on psychological trauma. Some of these methods are relatively inexpensive and easy to propagate, while others require more clinical expertise. The work of the Center for Mind-Body Medicine is particularly noteworthy in aggregating the best evidence-based methods and building programs, and their goal is to train thousands to heal millions.[6]

What if instead of focusing on expensive military interventions we were to support the instruction of a few thousand trauma-resolution trainers to spend two years each in the Middle

East doing free trainings for people in every major country? The goal would be to build more capacity with local leaders to heal the roots of trauma in the body, emotions, and minds of the population so that those roots don't fester into the next war. This could be led from the United Nations as part of its development work. It would be a group of skilled professionals who are spending their time to help cultures address the trauma that can be transmitted even intergenerationally. This effectively addresses the roots of violence and aggression in the region for a fraction of the cost of even one military intervention.

The fifth area to shift is to put more resources into the long-term economic and social development of the region. The ultimate solution to Middle East instability is to foster healthy cultures in which there is real opportunity for advancement and creating a better life for one's children. Cultural evolution is necessarily a slow process. We can help by fostering education, exchange, and business development in some of the most afflicted zones of violence and thus contribute to the creation of more resilient cultures. The more we can lend our skills and expertise in culture building wherever they are requested, the more we can help the Middle East become a thriving place that has moved beyond its bloody history.

While some of the development work has to happen on a government level, we can also take important steps on our own. For instance, when I first began this chapter I decided to make a microloan to three women entrepreneurs in Lebanon through Kiva, a remarkable organization. This tiny act, which took only five minutes, can help build a bridge of compassion that erodes prejudice. While writing the rest of the book, I added nine more loans to entrepreneurs in Iraq, Jordan, Yemen, Palestine, and Pakistan. Twenty-five dollars to each of these entrepreneurs is a tiny loan for me, but it can have a big impact when combined with loans from others. And perhaps more importantly, it sends a signal that another American honors them and wants to help them thrive.

I encourage each of us to consider a way that we reach out to Middle East brothers and sisters with a hand of friendship or support, whether that is through microloans, travel, or offers of face-to-face friendship. As I conclude editing this chapter, I decided to add another $225 worth of loans to entrepreneurs in Palestine, which only took a few minutes. While these actions can seem small, they add up to big changes when enough of us do them. As of this writing, Kiva has processed loans of $11,873,300 to entrepreneurs in Palestine alone. If we assume an average loan size of $1,500, that means there have been loans to approximately 8,000 entrepreneurs.[7]

Just think about the social impact of that for a moment. If the average Palestinian has a friendship network of around 150 people, that means that with 1.7 million people in the West Bank perhaps half are likely to be friends with someone who has received a loan from Kiva to grow a business, refurbish a house, or navigate a family crisis. Fifteen hundred dollars may not sound like a lot, but when the GDP is only $2,900 per person, $1,500 can mean the difference between creating a business that serves others and the spiral that leads to violence. The amount of goodwill and cultural evolution these little acts of empowerment create can't be overestimated, especially when compared to the lasting damage and animosity from one bombing campaign. Plus, it's virtually free, with only a bit over 1 percent of the loans ending in default. These small guerrilla acts of kindness and mutual respect can begin to soften the relationships beneath the surface, and I'll explore the power of this microfinance revolution and how to leverage it globally more in a later chapter.

The final area for improvement is perhaps the most obvious and the trickiest, which is the transformation of the Israel and Palestine conflict. I will not propose a specific political solution here except to say that we need to take into account the very real needs of all sides and to call for a resolution that provides safety for Israel and justice for Palestinians and that is backed by the United Nations for legitimacy. Beyond the political process, we should foster more collaborations that bridge the cultural divides, such as those undertaken by the Abrahamic Reunion of Jerusalem Peace-makers, which has Jewish, Muslim, and Christian leaders who do unorthodox forms of activism like the Jerusalem Hug, an inter-faith event that encircles the Old City every year.

At the Parliament of the World's Religions in 2015, I sat in on a session with a dozen or so leaders from this remarkable group, all of whom embrace each other with real love and partici-pate in shared meals, celebrations, weddings, and more. One of the respected leaders on the Arab Muslim side is Ibrahim Abu el-Hawa, who shared with Jewish leader Eliyahu McLean the story of an escalating situation in East Jerusalem, with a house being bull-dozed. As protestors gathered, it was about to turn violent before Ibrahim arrived and walked between Israeli soldiers and Arab protestors, declaring there would be no violence that day. Right at the most tense moment, an Israeli soldier recognized that he and Ibrahim had attended the same wedding of their mutual friend the previous weekend as a result of the Abrahamic Reunion work. The tension broke and there was no violence that day.

These kinds of cultural bridges are essential and can be built virtually as well, such as with shared media online. I've had the idea for a Holy Land TV, produced on both sides of the divide, modeled after successful work in Africa led by Search for Common Ground that has been used to prevent civil wars and heal cultural divides. There are great groups in Jerusalem working on bringing children who are Jewish, Muslim, and Christian together for camps, arts programs, and more. It's essential to foster these "soft" interven-tions to help clear the ancient wounds and entrenched fears that have resulted in so many hardened hearts and a diminishment of trust. Negotiated settlements are clearly part of transforming the Israel and Palestine situation, but so is finding a language of the heart that reconnects us into one family again. When that happens, it is far easier to find higher ground.

Ending Global Warming

The maltreatment of the natural world and its impoverishment leads to
the impoverishment of the human soul. To save the natural world today
means to save what is human in humanity.
—Raisa Gorbachev

As I write this chapter, global leaders have just emerged from the 2015 United Nations Climate Change Conference in Paris, which created the most significant progress yet to unify the world around preventing the massive damage from climate change that is predicted if we fail to prevent global temperatures from rising two degrees Celsius.

While the agreement forged is far from complete and ultimately is nonbinding, it does represent a historic attempt for our world community to address perhaps our most ominous collective challenge. The language of the agreement not only ratified the 2-degree cap but also pointed us toward the more ambitious 1.5-degree target, which would effectively mean getting to a world with zero net carbon pollution by 2050 and essentially transitioning from fossil fuels almost entirely. That goal is bold, but possible, and far more likely to prevent the most damaging effects of global warming.

The good news is that the United States has been making progress on reducing carbon pollution while still growing our economy since 2009. We've been reducing our carbon pollution annually by 1.2 percent, a rate that will increase to 2.3–2.8 percent per year from 2020 to 2028, leading to economy-wide reductions of 80 percent by 2050.[1] Those numbers are important because we start to recognize that ending global warming is only a 2–3 percent improvement per year issue. That starts to make it seem far more achievable, especially as renewable-energy production is beginning to scale more rapidly and electric-car technology is hitting the mainstream.

The long-term danger from global warming is clearly enormous and very expensive, with the potential to devastate economies, inundate farmland, trigger droughts, drive species into extinction, and dislocate large portions of the world's population, with a worst-case scenario of hundreds of millions starving. Prevention of these scenarios is well worth the effort. But part of the challenge in solving this problem is the sheer number of ways that we participate in it, from heating our homes to driving our cars to shipping our products from China. It's a very complex problem.

There is no one-stop solution for eliminating the carbon pollution that is driving global warming. However, there is a single *principle* that can help us create the many solutions required: every single one of us eventually has to take full responsibility for our own contribution to global warming. If we each paid a little bit to offset the carbon output created by driving our cars, heating our houses, and other lifestyle choices, that money could go to entrepreneurs and companies that develop innovative ways to remove carbon and other greenhouse gases from the atmosphere or to shift energy production to non-CO_2 sources. The end result of full personal responsibility translated into public policy would eventually be to halt global warming completely. This is the logic behind a so-called "carbon tax," but I think the logic behind a tax on carbon tends to trigger negative reactions for conservatives and Republicans.

Instead of focusing on a tax going to the government, we should focus on this being a Climate Responsibility Fee that means companies selling fossil fuels must then use that money to buy carbon offsets to neutralize the effect of the burning of the fossil fuels consumed. Calling it a Climate Responsibility Fee makes it clear exactly what it is and appeals to conservative values more; it's a way for us to take personal responsibility for our impacts on others.

The carbon offsets that are purchased by fossil-fuel-selling companies would go directly to entrepreneurs and companies who are figuring out creative ways to remove greenhouse gases from the atmosphere, improve efficiencies, and switch to sustainable fuels. Carbon offsets are thus a way to empower more entrepreneurship, which in turn creates more jobs.

The key to making personal climate responsibility a reality is that we can't rely on good intentions and voluntary choice alone. Eventually, we'll have to build it into the price structure so that market forces can drive us toward long-term solutions. For example, let's look at the impact of driving our cars. The average vehicle in America generates about five tons of CO_2 each year. Buying a high-quality carbon offset for this amount of carbon (such as when a new wind farm comes online) would cost fifty to sixty dollars for the entire year, or about five dollars per month. Now, we can spend a lot of time and money educating people about the virtues of driving less or buying an electric car. Or we could simply add a Climate Responsibility Fee to every gallon of gas that someone purchases, which might be ten to twenty cents per gallon of gas. After a number of price surges in recent years, it is clear that we have the capability to absorb higher gasoline prices fairly quickly, increase our transportation fleet's fuel efficiency, and not significantly hinder the economy. Especially if phased in over time, twenty cents per gallon is quite reasonable when the end result is avoiding massive global climate change and the enormous expenses that will generate.

The benefit of the pay-as-you-go personal climate solution is that it becomes easy and invisible to consumers while creating an enormous business opportunity for innovative approaches that remove excess carbon and other greenhouse gases. For example, if someone did a reforestation project and received carbon offset certificates for each tree planted, it might make the reforestation of a clear-cut forest financially desirable as well as good for the planet. Committed green entrepreneurs would have many new career options. Someone living in the desert might have enough land and sun to install a small solar thermal generation plant and fund it from carbon offsets. City dwellers might receive an extra credit for installing wind turbines on their roofs. Urban workers might be paid to retrofit businesses and reduce their energy use. And so on.

The cost to individual consumers of a Climate Responsibility Fee would be on the order of five to twenty dollars per month but be virtually invisible because it would be embedded in the price of gas, energy, and other goods. More importantly, the incentives would empower the transition to less carbon-intensive forms of renewable energy. For example, what if an individual homeowner were able to get cash up front for carbon credits when a rooftop solar array is installed? Let's say this solar array would remove three hundred metric tons of CO_2 from electricity grid production over the next thirty years. The homeowner might get \$3,000 of credit for the installation up front. With new financing programs, a solarized citizen could spread the cost of the equipment over ten or twenty years. So he or she might actually make money on the installation and pay market electrical rates or better for the next twenty years, which would provide the cost competitiveness necessary to drive significant new adoption.

And this is not even taking into account the massive solar leasing programs that now allow many homeowners to add solar with no money down and pay on a monthly basis, sometimes at a lower rate than the conventional electrical grid. There are also exciting new financing options under way, such as that led by the energy financing company Ygrene, which have made it so that energy use enhancements can be added to our property tax bill and paid off over time (or passed on to the next owner).

These sorts of positive market-based feedback loops will become even more rapid as we create an ever-larger carbon offset market through mandatory climate protection fees on those things that generate greenhouse gases. Eventually, the principle of each of us taking personal responsibility for our contribution to climate change can become as American as apple pie.

Before such an approach can be implemented in America as a whole, it will probably first need to be successfully demonstrated in a single place. The most natural fit for a demonstration project would be California, which has the most green-positive political climate, the world's seventh largest economy, the strongest clean-tech venture industry, as well as media and Internet companies that can engage the grass roots.

In California, the goal of becoming a fully carbon-neutral state would require offsetting approximately 350 million metric tons of carbon.[2] At roughly $10 per metric ton for a high-quality offset, that would create a $3.7 billion per year market for people who develop offsets for those carbon emissions—an enormous market opportunity.

Grassroots citizen engagement will be vital to build the political will to become the first carbon-neutral state. Certain groups have talked about this as a "California moonshot," and it can probably be done in a decade with sufficient political will. California's role as a leader of innovation would make it more attractive for other states to follow. The strategy would thus focus on building a Carbon-Neutral California campaign.

A Carbon-Neutral California campaign could begin by creating a web-based social network, which would become a "citizen network" for people who have made the voluntary commitment to offset their own carbon. Members would join a monthly membership program, at least half of which would go toward buying personal carbon offsets. Another percentage would go to nonprofits doing supportive work, and a final percentage would pay for site media, educational programs, infrastructure development, outreach, and eventually lobbying efforts for carbon neutral legislation. One website could thus become a comprehensive engine to empower the collective shift to carbon neutrality.

The way I see it, in the early stages of a Carbon-Neutral California campaign, four activities of the campaign could build on each other:

- Personal voluntary offsets

- Events

- Organizational offsets

- Lobbying and grassroots mobilization

The target goal for the campaign would be to eventually offset the entire current output for California of 353 million tons of CO_2 every year, while also leading to reductions in output. In this way, California would become the first economy in the world to zero out its carbon and demonstrate that it is possible while still growing the economy.

Carbon Neutral California marketing campaigns might focus on California's pride in creating the future—the future of technology, entertainment, business, societal change movements, etc. Its messaging would thus focus on California having the opportunity to be the first major economy in the world to fully address global warming by reducing carbon dioxide output and by offsetting the remainder. These awareness campaigns would then be tethered to messaging focused around how we positively influence the world, which in turn would benefit tourism and our business climate.

As a California campaign gains momentum, we could challenge other states to beat us to the prize of being the first carbon-neutral state. In this way, the Carbon Neutral California campaign would harness competitive instincts, media, and strategic campaigns to shift the psychology around offsets and create an innovative social network that can drive political efforts, as well as local engagement.

I believe it is possible for us to end global warming by 2050 and possibly even earlier. The key principle is taking personal responsibility for our own contribution to global warming and then unleashing entrepreneurship for the innovation required, which can result in political and policy changes at state, national, and then global levels. Whichever state leads the way politically to create the legislation, market forces can then drive a more widespread shift toward personal climate responsibility, which can work in concert with grassroots networks to support a policy shift to a climate-friendly economy.

Uplifting through Microfinance

When will our consciences grow so tender that we will act to
prevent human misery rather than avenge it?
—Eleanor Roosevelt

ONE OF THE MOST fundamental facts that contributes to conflict in the world is the global gap between the haves and the have-nots; in 2014, Oxfam released a study that showed that the richest 85 people in the world had the same wealth as the bottom 3.8 billion and 10 percent of the world's population holds 86 percent of all wealth.[1] This problem may not seem to be "our" problem. If other countries can't develop thriving economies, that's their problem—or so the more isolationist thinking goes.

Seen from a higher vantage point, though, the picture is different. The health of the entire world is increasingly interdependent. Pollution in China affects the US fishing industry. Deforestation in Brazil can contribute to drought in the Midwest. Slums in Calcutta may be catalysts for global pandemics. And failed political states can become breeding grounds for terrorists. America's self-interest is thus increasingly intertwined with the interests of all the world's people.

From a sacred perspective, we are all working together on the project of co-creating a better world. For us to act in a way that undermines the health and well-being of our brothers and sisters undermines not only them but also ourselves. We become more alienated from our hearts and more disconnected from the well-spring of joy in us. We cannot live from our highest potential while we contribute to the suffering of others.

It's thus imperative for an America 7.0 to be one in which we are catalysts for creating a world in which we eradicate poverty. The engine of capitalism tends to drive more and more resources to those who already have the most. It's thus incumbent upon those living in relative affluence to creatively engage the task of helping the rest of the world lift itself out of poverty.

Playing our part in helping the rest of the world become more self-sufficient need not be an excessive burden. It can be a great joy. I'm thinking of the inspiring story of Shana Chrystie, a vice president of operations at the travel company Geographic Expeditions. At the end of 2007, she listened to a teleseminar with Jessica Jackley, a cofounder of the microfinance nonprofit Kiva. Kiva builds a personal bridge of connection to developing world entrepreneurs in more than eighty countries, with lenders offering them a few hundred to a few thousand dollars to start or grow small businesses. From this simple concept, Kiva has grown into an organization that has brokered more than $757 million in loans from 1,340,000 lenders to 1,751,000 entrepreneurs in eighty-three developing countries. When loans are repaid—as 98.5 percent are—most people choose to re-loan their money to a new entrepreneur. So the benefit of the money can be multiplicative.

When Shana heard about Kiva's remarkable program, she convinced her company to skip its traditional holiday packages of fancy chocolate and instead make twenty-five-dollar gifts to Kiva in each of its clients' names. Clients could then make a loan to an entrepreneur of their choice in the developing world: a goat herder in Tajikistan, a seamstress in Uganda, a weaver in Bolivia—whoever inspired them the most.

The effect was truly remarkable:

We have never before had such heartwarming responses to our holiday gifts! One couple had never heard of Kiva before, but upon investigation were so impressed that they switched some of their holiday gifts for friends and family over to Kiva gift certificates. Another expressed his hope that he could take his family to visit his loan recipient. More than one said that our gift was one of the "best ideas of the season." And for our staff & management, giving this gift has been one of our most deeply gratifying experiences.

The ripple effect of this kind of philanthropy is remarkable. Let's estimate that Geographic Expedition's holiday gifts were used for loans to one hundred different entrepreneurs in the first year. As each of those entrepreneurs pulls themselves out of poverty, they likely lift their immediate families with them, which may be four or five people. As the network of entrepreneurism grows in their village or community, there are further positive effects on the local economy. So let's imagine the first round of microloans benefits five hundred people. As the loans are repaid, often within a year, the money can be re-loaned, such that over ten years the original gift might directly benefit five thousand people. That's a remarkable effect from one act of corporate giving.

Perhaps more importantly, by pioneering a new kind of corporate giving, Geographic Expeditions is inspiring its clients to join in, and other companies may well follow suit. One person's idea may thus have a positive effect on tens of thousands of people in the coming decade. And the great beauty is that people in the developing world are not receiving charity but funds to become more self-reliant, which is far more effective long term. Finally, the Kiva loans were actually less expensive than the previous year's holiday packages, which meant Geographic Expeditions saved money while creating a wave of goodwill and philanthropy. Now that's the kind of innovative generosity that can truly change the world!

On a psychological level, direct person-to-person microloans help weave the world together and contribute to making war and terrorism obsolete. Let's say that a teenage boy in Pakistan is exposed, on the one hand, to a negative story about the evils of America, but on the other he hears his aunt sing the praises of lenders who funded her sewing business that is now feeding her children and allowing her to save money for their education. The power of the negative story about Americans will effectively be mitigated by the story of the aunt who was able to launch a small business with loans from Americans. Instead of channeling his frustration with America into destructive acts, that teenage boy is more likely to come up with a business plan and seek a loan himself.

Microloans are thus a more effective and personal form of foreign policy than bombs. And they are far less expensive. As microlending surges in popularity, it could be that the American government shifts money from the defense budget into large microlending funds to support developing world entrepreneurs. The $10 billion spent on a state-of-the-art warship might instead empower four million grassroots entrepreneurs with $500 microloans. It would be especially powerful to do this in partnership with US citizens, so that each citizen loan could be matched by federal money. This would keep the personal bridge of connection but harness a larger pool of resources. People might even be given the option of having a percentage of their taxes go into a microloan pool that they manage themselves.

In this way, $10 billion from the federal government could be paired with $10 billion from American citizens in a way that empowers eight million new entrepreneurs every year, who each in turn support families and villages. The economic benefit of this shift would be vast, offering an extremely powerful way to not only lift the world out of poverty but also sow the seeds for a prosperous global culture. We'd have one less warship but be a whole lot closer to a safe world because the truth is that economic hardship and violence go hand in hand. The most serious terrorism threats emerge from deeply broken economies and collapsed states.

Kiva is not the only game in town (or the only solution). Another organization that I've been involved with is the Foundation for International Community Assistance (FINCA), which sponsors village banks that become self-sustaining lenders to the previously unbanked poor. We've contributed to the creation of village banks in four countries. One of the really exciting things I've learned from FINCA is that it is participating in a larger campaign to get every adult who is not currently banked—currently two billion people, or almost one in three adults—to have access to basic banking by the year 2020. While it sounds audacious to reach two billion people, the last three years have resulted in seven hundred million new people getting access to basic banking services.[2] So two billion more in the next five years *is* an achievable goal as momentum builds and the enabling technologies become ever more ubiquitous. It's particularly valuable to have a basic banking foundation in place for very poor people. Once they have access to credit and savings, they are better able to weather the storms of life, as well as build sustainable sources of income and microenterprises that take care of their families. They can gradually obtain clean water, sanitation, electricity, housing, education, and health care. In short, they can make a reasonable life for themselves. This is ultimately far more effective than handouts.

A sacred America is one that truly cares for the whole, including the downtrodden and the destitute, both at home and abroad. By lending a helping hand up so that even people in the bottom two billion can become financially self-sufficient and entrepreneurial, we also build bridges of compassion, gratitude, and mutual respect, which are ultimately the best form of defense.

The Sacred Corporation

A business that makes nothing but money is a poor business.
—Henry Ford

NEXT I WANT TO address one of the real friction points between the left and right, which has to do with a key engine of capitalism: the corporation. Those on the left tend to have a deep distrust of corporations, whereas there's an almost religious celebration of big business by the right and a belief that it will do good if simply left unfettered.

On the left, the reasoning goes that corporations are designed to only maximize shareholder value, which encourages them to be amoral, ruthless, and predatory, unless strictly controlled by regulations. Because the largest companies operate beyond the constraints and rules of any single nation, they tend to play different nations off each other, driving the global workforce toward lower wages and lower environmental standards. Some of the biggest are now "too big to fail" and are further protected by the Supreme Court rulings that gave corporations the same rights as persons. Finally, corporations pay lobbyists that actively seek to distort our political process and bend legislation to their advantage.

This view leads to the logical conclusion on the left that corporations must be redesigned, dramatically downsized, or eliminated.

However, what if everything has been created for a higher purpose but it has not yet found its highest expression? I believe that the right's reverence for corporate success is founded on a real recognition of the sacred and dynamic power intrinsic in capitalism. If we can combine reforms that address the left's critiques with the admiration that informs the right's stance, I believe we can harness the power of corporations for the greater good in a much deeper way.

Corporations are excellent at the rapid creation of value. We have no social structures that can move as quickly or as effectively to deal with new market conditions. Those companies that linger in the past quickly lose market share, which means companies are forced to create change in a way that religions, social institutions, and governments cannot. Even while they have often been purveyors of environmental and social problems, in the years ahead I believe corporations will be the workhorses that drive the positive economic and cultural shifts ahead of us if we can simply realign some incentives.

Seen from a higher perspective, the corporation is one of our most efficient engines for creativity, for it is designed to harvest the best work of sometimes hundreds of thousands of people in order to serve a market need. If people will not pay for a good or service, the corporation moves quickly in a new direction rather than wasting energy on something that does not generate a profit. In this sense, they are our most sensitive evolutionary indicator: What is in demand now? How are we growing in our needs? What is important to our country at the moment?

When we see everything as sacred, market needs are themselves holy in a certain way—market demand calls forth our creative potential, with money as the reward for delivering something of value more efficiently than anyone else. That is why so many Americans, particularly on the right, revere the free market—there is a deep-seated belief in the natural creative power that is intrinsic in free economic activity. That view offers important truths that people on the left especially need to hear and understand.

What is also true, though, is that this picture distorts in a number of places. First, on the consumer end, when people are less conscious, they often desire things that are not good for them or the world. This is a demand-side distortion. There is clearly a very real demand for illicit drugs. There's a demand for child prostitutes. There's a demand for cigarettes. There's a demand for many things that are destructive to the fabric of our culture or that impinge on health and happiness or that lead people into addictive spirals. This is where government has a rightful role to protect the masses against the destructive activities of the few. Corporations that profit from life-negating, addictive, or exploitative activities often will use effective marketing to generate more demand for their products, as well as fight legislative controls. Protecting our citizens from this kind of negative social impact is important and can be accomplished by regulation, which prevents consumers from buying life-negating products, or taxation, which drives down consumer demand on unhealthy products.

Second, on the corporate end, there is a tendency to hide or externalize the real costs of production—human, environmental, or other—and to instead use deceptive advertising to portray a rosier picture. Companies have a vested interest in keeping their production costs low, which can result in social and environmental damage where products are made, all beneath the shiny veneer of beautiful packaging, often hawked by a beloved athlete. In other words, corporations are currently incentivized to take less conscious and even unethical actions behind closed doors while maintaining a rosy public facade. The key principle to transform this aspect of corporate misbehavior is *transparency*; the more we know about corporations' behaviors, the more effectively citizens in the market can reward them for good actions and punish them for bad actions.

If we take this principle to the next, most logical level, what we will eventually want to create is a global system of corporate responsibility ratings, assessed by an independent body and made visible on every product that is sold. These Conscious Ratings Tags would go beyond "green" seals or "fair trade" stamps, which are great preliminary ways to reward companies for good behavior. Under this system, companies would have assessments of multiple areas of ethical practices, from their treatment of labor to their practices of sustainability, each with a score from one to ten, giving them the incentives for continuous improvement and excellence. Just as we now have nutrition labels that make the contents of our food more transparent (which was a major innovation itself), so would every product have a label with ratings of company practices.

Conscious Ratings Tags would ultimately be more effective than regulation in harnessing the positive evolutionary power of corporations. Company improvements in any area that resulted in higher ratings overall would allow them to charge higher prices, expand market share, or receive extra investment from socially responsible investment funds. A socially responsible fund might, for instance, only invest in companies with an average rating of seven or better out of ten.

Such a rating system would encourage a greater focus on all those social and environmental impacts that are normally not transparent to the consumer. High-performing employees would also prefer working for highly rated companies, and discerning consumers would patronize those businesses. So a company moving up in the ratings system would result in a short-term return on investment (ROI) from customers, a medium-term ROI from investors, and a long-term ROI from attracting and retaining top talent. These kinds of financial ROIs drive the most rapid innovations. The only way this works effectively and efficiently, though, is if it is fully transparent to the end user, especially when they are making their buying decisions.

When ethical, life-affirming choices become more profitable for corporations than unethical, life-negating choices, corporations will rapidly become the leaders of innovation in every single area of social improvement simply because they are designed to follow profit. If we orient a corporate responsibility system to make ethical behavior more visible to consumers, investors, and employees and therefore more profitable, there will be a vast, competitive landscape of do-gooder corporations competing for market share.

In many ways, this is the natural extension of trends already in place. We have socially responsible investment screens that allow investors to participate only in companies that maintain a certain standard. We have Energy Star tags for appliances, highway-mileage ratings for cars, and fair-trade certification for coffees. We have a raft of sustainability report cards and initiatives that now drive corporate innovation. With the omnipresence of social media, it is clearly essential for companies to maintain a trustworthy corporate brand. The next step is to ensure that companies go beyond image to actual excellence in their treatment of their workers, their communities, and the environment as well as commit to creating excellent products.

To harness the full evolutionary, creative power of the corporate engine for good, then, requires working from both ends of the economic exchange to ensure that the products available for purchase are non-harmful to consumers and society and that there are no hidden damages involved in the production of those goods. The end result of incentivizing both of these behaviors simultaneously is that we gain full, conscious knowledge of the implications of our economic decisions. As we do that, the most conscious and highest-integrity corporations win—as do we as a society—thus taking the concept of win-win-win to a higher level.

The final ingredient to unleashing more of the evolutionary potential of corporations is a fair playing field that ensures that when companies win, it is because of their ability to serve a real human need with excellence and without undermining the society. We've already created laws making it clear that slave labor is no longer acceptable. Nor is child labor. Nor is paying below a minimum wage. The next level of this movement toward positive work regulations is to ensure that every person who is working full time can do so *without* government assistance, which effectively acts as a subsidy for businesses that pay ultralow wages.

I recently watched a sobering video of what it is like for a single mother to live on a $7.50 minimum-wage job at McDonald's. It was grim. The video made it clear just how many government subsidies for rent, childcare, food, and more this woman needed just to survive. And even with that support, she still was forced to make very hard choices, such as getting a tooth pulled rather than have a root canal because she had no extra money in her budget. In essence, what is happening in her case is that McDonald's and its shareholders are getting the full economic benefits of her labor while paying her below what it actually takes for her to live. We the taxpayers are then paying to subsidize the difference through government subsidies. So in the final analysis we, as taxpayers, are subsidizing McDonald's shareholders by helping to underwrite their low-wage workers. That situation should be outrageous, especially to conservatives who believe in smaller government and personal responsibility!

At the lowest, entry-level, low-skill jobs there will always be a strong downward push on wages. Many of these businesses will effectively go to the absolute limit of how much the government (in other words, we, the taxpayers) will subsidize their workers. If they can push some of the cost of their employees on to us, they will.

The federal minimum wage should thus be set at a level that allows workers to fulfill their most basic human needs for food, shelter, clothing, and health care without *any* government assistance. People should be able to be self-sufficient, even if their life is quite modest, rather than dependent on the government (and therefore the rest of us) when they are working forty hours a week. So long as our minimum wage is set so low that government assistance is actually required for full-time workers to make ends meet, we end up with a larger welfare state and a larger drain on the resources of middle-class taxpayers and companies that pay higher wages.

The irony of the minimum wage debate is that Republicans want to reduce the size of the welfare state and government programs but don't recognize that raising the minimum wage to a level that allows subsistence living at a minimum wage is essential to reduce the size of the government and taxes. A fair floor for wages allows market forces to work their magic and the best companies to succeed without depending on government/taxpayer handouts, as they currently do.

On the Democratic side of the ledger, there's been a strong push for a higher minimum wage, moving up to $10.10 per hour or the more ambitious goal of $15 per hour (which is still probably just barely at a level at which people can live without government subsidies), but their messaging tends to focus on workers' rights and compassion rather than reducing the size of government subsidies and reducing tax burden for others—logic that would appeal more to conservatives.

Ultimately, raising the minimum wage to a true living wage is about self-responsibility, which is a core conservative principle— requiring companies to pay people at a level that is not subsidized by others makes the companies self-responsible and the employees self-responsible, which also makes them feel better about their lives. And the truth is that because most businesses are competing in similar markets, a higher minimum wage does not undermine their ability to compete for market share—everyone has the same minimum cost of labor.

So a higher minimum wage can advance the goals of both major political parties, but the current messaging turns it into a class warfare issue rather than a source of bipartisan alignment. Messaging that appeals directly to more conservative values and priorities will likely get more traction than trying to win people over with messages that appeal only to traditionally liberal values.

Many companies are now recognizing that a higher minimum wage actually directly benefits them as well because paying employees at that rate makes them happier, healthier, and more resilient, which lifts the culture of the business and improves the public perception of their brand. By setting the minimum wage at a level that doesn't force the rest of society to subsidize workers, we create a more dynamic economy in which the most productive and high-value-generating companies are not underwriting those that are bottom-feeding.

At The Shift Network, we made the decision to raise our minimum annual salary to $50,000 for staff who are beyond an entry-level period, even for roles that are traditionally paid much less, such as customer support. The main benefit, besides a clear conscience, is that our team members are able to take care of themselves and show up in a happy, healthy, positive way, which creates a more resilient culture with very low turnover. We don't have to deal with much negativity because our team members have what I call a "self-actualizing wage" that allows them to be on a path of health, personal growth, and realizing their dreams. With the safety net of health insurance and a 401(k) retirement savings account, our staff have the basics covered, which reduces the amount of worry, stress, and existential fear.

And we're far from the leaders in this arena, as Gravity Payments in Seattle became globally famous in 2015 when its CEO Dan Price cut his own pay by 90 percent and boosted the company minimum salary to $70,000 (to be phased in over several years). This action provoked quite a lot of controversy, but ultimately it has led to growth for the business. Since the announcement, revenues are twice what they were before the move, and profits have also doubled.[1]

In Silicon Valley, our company benefits are actually less than what the biggest companies use to attract top talent. The Googles,

Facebooks, and Apples of the world have 24/7 food, gyms, professional bodyworkers, nap chairs, education programs, long parental leave, and much more. While not every company can emulate these perks when they are small startups, the trajectory is clear: when a company takes excellent care of its employees, it creates a more positive, creative, and successful culture with lower turnover that is more attractive to top talent.

It's actually an enjoyable and creative process to think of new benefits that aren't necessarily expensive but meet a real need our team members have. For example, we recently added a "global work" benefit that allows staff to work one month out of the year while living in another country, provided they keep a regular workweek and maintain their responsibilities. This will allow our team to explore more of the world—something many of them expressed as a dream—without needing long vacations.

There are many exciting movements under way for "conscious capitalism," "triple bottom line business, " and "B corporations," all of which orient companies to become better citizens of our world and make a more positive impact as part of their mission. We've hosted four Enlightened Business Summits online that have featured innovative leaders such as Tony Hsieh at Zappos, John Mackey at Whole Foods, and Chip Conley from Joie de Vivre Hospitality. What is inspiring about these innovators is that they are focused on building self-actualizing corporate cultures while also serving up great products. They are trying to do good and do well at the same time—and succeeding with flying colors! *Fortune* puts out an annual 100 Best Companies to Work For list, and an independent study by the Russell Investment Group found they outperformed the S&P 500 index by an average of two to one.[2] And what is really interesting is that forward-looking companies are now competing on culture because of the long-term market advantage. Every company wants to be known as one that offers great conditions.

The same principles can apply to mom-and-pop operations to mid-level companies to the Fortune 500. It's a truly exciting time for the evolution of "sacred commerce," a term coined by Matthew and Terces Engelheart, the founders of the successful Café Gratitude chain that combines healthy cuisine with a dose of positive psychology.

Some of the most promising developments are when companies embed their philanthropy right into their sales. For instance, Toms Shoes gives a pair of shoes away in the developing world for *every* pair they sell, which is remarkable.

While market forces and investors are still often pushing corporations toward short-term profit maximization, there's an increasing recognition that, in the age of increasing transparency and social media, no one benefits (including shareholders) when a company becomes known for exploitation and negative impact in the world. It's demoralizing for workers and damaging to the brand. All that remains is for us to take the natural migration toward more transparency and a higher baseline of social responsibility to the next level where companies are all competing to become the best across the board and really leave a legacy of good.

With more information at our disposal, and with a growing number of educated citizens, the engine of capitalism can drive us even more rapidly toward a thriving world. Our current version of commerce will increasingly become sacred commerce—business that honors people, planet, and profits and that empowers the creation of a more enlightened world. We can then more fully celebrate the corporation (even the large ones!) as one of the great innovations of humankind, allowing us to turn individual creativity and ingenuity into forces for good that benefit, evolve, and enlighten humankind.

And that is one of the greatest gifts America can give the world: a roaring capitalist engine that is also socially responsible and just.

Transforming Our Banking System

*If the American people ever allow private banks to control the
issue of their currency, first by inflation, then by deflation, the
banks and corporations that will grow up around (these banks)
will deprive the people of all property until their children wake up
homeless on the continent their fathers conquered.*

—Thomas Jefferson

TO FOSTER THE EMERGENCE of America 7.0, one of the key areas
that will need an upgrade is our banking system because it is directly
related to our mountainous debt, an issue that threatens to cripple
our future and is the cause of so much partisan warfare and strife.

While we take it for granted that the federal government has
simply spent beyond its means, there's a deeper layer of this story
that goes to the heart of how money is actually created in our country (and how it could be in the future). For those who have peered
behind the curtain of our financial system and glimpsed its inner
workings, it can be a shock. It is sometimes likened to the book
The Wonderful Wizard of Oz, and for good reason: that story was written by Frank Baum as an allegory for the corrupted workings of
our financial system when he was a committed activist on the matter in the late 1890s. The characters and symbolism connect with
issues such as the gold standard, the exploitation of workers, and

solutions such as Dorothy's silver shoes, which were a metaphor for the coining of money by our government.

Upgrading our financial system is something that can become transpartisan common ground, for the hidden truths are offensive to both conservative and progressive value systems. While this distortion lingers, the next evolution of America will be impeded since the financial system itself will continue to act corrosively on the foundations of our democracy.

While there are many great investigations and books that offer well-researched details about our banking system, in this chapter I want to explore just a few key elements of what we all need to know, drawn from Ellen Brown's highly recommended *Web of Debt*. So here is the surprising backstory of our banking system that goes to the heart of the problem.

First, the most important piece of information is that the Federal Reserve is not owned by the federal government. It is actually a privately held corporation owned by a collection of banks and, through them, wealthy financiers. And there are no actual reserves in the Federal Reserve. Money is created out of thin air as a result of making entries in ledgers on computers.

Our government or other banks gain access to this "debt-money" by borrowing it, with interest, which taxpayers then eventually must repay, creating profit for those who created the money and a mounting debt for our nation (or other banks and eventually people).

Historically, there was a battle over the right of nations to create their own form of debt-free money. Before the American Revolution, individual states issued their own paper currencies and experienced considerable affluence, as had been true in many countries that issued their own currency. The English government shut down this practice and started taxing American goods, payable only in gold and silver, which threw America into an economic depression as the money supply shrank. This helped to provide the kindling that sparked the American Revolution.

During the revolution, paper money called continentals were created to fund the war but were then attacked by speculators while Britain flooded the market with counterfeits in an attempt to undermine the currency. The ability to print our own money was perceived as a dire threat that needed to be addressed with acts of financial warfare.

After the war and the devaluation of the currency, treasury secretary Alexander Hamilton felt that he needed to get the wealthy class on board with the creation of a new monetary system and thus gave away the nation's right to create money to a new private institution, the shares of which were sold.

Several later presidents such as Andrew Jackson and Abraham Lincoln challenged this situation and attempted to dissolve the central bank's charter and return to state-issued money, which resulted in a form of economic warfare. Jackson did succeed for a time, and the nation was free of debt. To finance the Civil War and implement powerful economic reforms, Lincoln developed greenbacks, again issued directly as legal tender by the state. In the long run, though, the private financiers regained control.

In 1913, the deceptively worded Federal Reserve Act slipped through Congress right before Christmas and without adequate review. While it appeared to provide some safeguards, it had actually been quietly crafted by some of the wealthiest and most powerful Americans to put in place a system of usury, giving the United States an ever-growing debt.

The story of Guernsey, seventy-five miles from Britain, is one of the few inspirations for how to avoid the trap of privately issued money through central banks that ensnares countries in debt. In 1816, the island's infrastructure was in disarray and it was heavily in debt, with many leaving for work elsewhere. Most of Guernsey's annual income went to interest on its debt. The government then began to issue its own interest-free notes in 1820, which paid for massive development of infrastructure and public works. It continued to issue new money regularly, but there was no inflation and the economy continued to grow rapidly. Today, Guernsey is prosperous, debt-free, and stable, with a relatively low flat income tax (20 percent) without loopholes. Guernsey remains a potent case study of the benefits of keeping control of the production of money in public hands and a strong counterargument to the fear and misinformation spread about the perils of such a path.

Building a truly sacred and prosperous America with a 7.0 operating system will require reforming our banking in substantial ways because the current structure is designed to foster scarcity and competition, which work at cross-purposes to a healthy economy built on oneness.

Bernard Lietaer, one of the architects of the euro and a deep thinker on money, said this in an interview:

> We can produce more than enough food to feed everybody, and there is definitely enough work for everybody in the world, but there is clearly not enough money to pay for it all. The scarcity is in our national currencies. In fact, the job of central banks is to create and maintain that currency scarcity. The direct consequence is that we have to fight with each other in order to survive.[1]

The ultimate solution is simple even if it is challenging to implement: the Federal Reserve system needs to be dissolved and the constitutional power to create debt-free money needs to be restored to our federal government subject to the will of the people through our representatives. While that is the end goal, the early stages of reform are more likely to happen on a local level first, through public state and city banks.

North Dakota offers the most inspiring example, even while the idea dates back to early Quakers who created a public bank in Pennsylvania. The real secret to North Dakota's booming economy and success is not shale oil but in having the only state-owned bank in the country, the Bank of North Dakota, which is beholden to its only shareholder, the people of the state. North Dakota had positive public balance sheets through the years after the 2009 financial crisis put most of the country into a tailspin, and it managed to reduce both personal income tax and property taxes during that time. It has returned $300 million to the state's general fund over the last decade, helping North Dakota's government to turn a surplus. By partnering with private banks, the Bank of North Dakota helped the state deliver the lowest foreclosure rate and lowest credit-card default rate in the country while the economy took off. The Bank of North Dakota effectively acts as its own mini Federal Reserve, supporting the work of other banks in the state.[2]

The key takeaway of the North Dakota success story is that change *can* happen at a state level, which can eventually build momentum for deep structural changes at the federal level. It's important to note that public banks can coexist peacefully with private banks, as is already the case in countries like Australia, Switzerland, Germany, India, China, and Brazil, which are further ahead on this issue than we are.

While the prospect of Federal Reserve reform may sound daunting, the pathway forward is for banking reform to begin with states creating their own banks before we build the momentum for the larger shift of the Federal Reserve to a US bank that issues money and can more effectively prevent the debt spirals that are crippling our future.

The key is getting enough people educated about the implications of our current system, as well as the pathway to a more abundant economy for future generations. To get involved and stay abreast of this movement, you can get engaged with the Public Banking Institute, which has become a hub for organizing local chapters and campaigns for state or local banks.

23

Solutions Councils

*A nation's strength ultimately consists in what it can do on
its own, and not in what it can borrow from others.*
—Indira Gandhi

I WANT TO CLOSE Part Three with the exploration of an idea that
goes beyond a single solution or policy to the creation of a new
structure of government that could help accelerate the emergence
and adoption of innovative solutions across the country.

A number of years ago, I had the idea that we could use a
new government structure that would focus on forward-looking
transpartisan solutions. Then, in discussions with author Barbara
Marx Hubbard, who had a parallel idea of a Peace Room in the
White House that tracks emerging innovations, I saw the potential for this to be implemented at the national level. The name that
came to me was a White House Solutions Council, which would
identify, harvest, and amplify innovations happening in each sector
of society. Whereas the Cabinet must focus on the most pressing
concerns of today, a Solutions Council could focus on the emergent innovations of tomorrow.

Solutions is a word that transcends the rhetoric of both left and
right to find true common ground. All of us are looking for solutions
that improve our country and solve real problems. Better awareness

of these emerging solutions could inform decision-making and thus help the president to build more strategically toward the future. I submitted this idea to the first Obama administration but did not hear back.

As I sat with this idea over the years and talked it over with another friend who ran for California State Senate, I eventually decided to share it with the current lieutenant governor of California, Gavin Newsom, thinking that it could be templated at a state level in California first. He quite liked the idea, and while it hasn't entered into reality yet, I remain convinced that the concept of Solutions Councils could be a major source of innovation in the governance of our country because they would be about a structure that allows the harvesting and replication of innovation, as well as grassroots, bottom-up participation.

The same structure could be applied at state, city, and even neighborhood levels, resulting in a network of Solutions Councils that can work synergistically with government from the local to the national level. Each Solutions Council would be tasked to scan the landscape for breakthrough solutions that can be scaled up or transform existing activities. Their task would be to think ahead of the curve and find the most successful, cost-efficient programs that can be implemented more widely.

This system of Solutions Councils could operate in parallel with elected officials to bring forward ideas that might otherwise be overlooked in the public process, as well as replicate innovative local programs in other areas of the country. They would provide a bottom-up and participatory process to complement top-down decision-making.

In identifying promising solutions, the two key requirements would be to find solutions that deliver better results *and* do so with lower costs. This dual nature is key to generating bipartisan appeal. Democrats often want to extend services to a broader range of people, and Republicans prefer smaller, leaner, more efficient government. Truly innovative solutions, then, will address both of these values simultaneously. Better results along with cost savings means these are innovations that we can't afford to ignore.

A Solutions Council could be constituted such that it will have representatives from each sector of a healthy society. Barbara Marx Hubbard and other allies have created a twelve-sector model for human society that she calls the Wheel of Co-Creation, which reflects a holistic way of seeing all the sectors of society working together. The twelve-sectored circle model also reflects the twelve-around-one structure that architectural genius Buckminster Fuller said offers an ideal design that mirrors the deep structure of the universe. The Solutions Council would build on this design with twelve representatives, one for each sector—justice, health, spirituality, infrastructure, environment, media, governance, relations, arts, economics, science, and education—thus reflecting the wholeness of our society.

Each council member and his or her staff would review groundbreaking ideas and programs, with a special focus on identifying those that accomplish the following:

- Have a track record of delivering superior results over time

- Leverage public, private, and nonprofit partnerships

- Create benefits in multiple areas

- Cost the same as or less than existing approaches

- Can be replicated

The best new solutions and strategies for implementation would be presented to either an interagency task force or directly to government officials for review and possible ratification.

A network of grassroots Solutions Councils could also invite participation through a web 2.0 platform that would encourage citizens to share, review, and advocate for breakthrough solutions in each domain and in each area of the country. Ratings and commentary would allow the best ideas from these citizen scouts to surface and be vetted through democratic participation, creating a more inclusive form of governance. In this way, we can forge a more participatory role for American citizens in the process of governance. Citizens would be able to co-create projects and policies rather than simply voting for their favorite candidate or party.

The way I am currently envisioning a Solutions Council would be to have sector chairs, each of whom is a respected leader in their domain. The chairs would oversee the work of a larger sector team consisting of domain experts. These teams would meet quarterly as a small group and between meetings engage in regular brainstorming and exchange. We would then convene a regular conference with the entire group to present the best innovations and identify opportunities for collaboration and synergy between the sectors and initiatives.

The Solutions Council would have a core staff with expertise in assessment, policy, and media work, as well as online organizing and business incubation. The online component of the Solutions Council would enable citizens to submit new ideas, as well as identify winning solutions. Policy staff would focus on developing the most promising solutions into coherent policies that could be implemented at the state level. And the media team would develop powerful and compelling cross-platform media around the best solutions so that each can be marketed effectively and shared with political leaders elsewhere. Finally, a business incubator wing could identify for-profit opportunities and partners for solutions so that they can be scaled as rapidly as possible.

With a small core staff harvesting the most innovative solutions from dozens of community leaders who are working across the full spectrum of society, a state-level Solutions Council could become a powerful engine for the evolution of one state and, even more importantly, an effective template for how we can accelerate inno-vation for our country as a whole. By demonstrating the power that can be harnessed not only from thought leaders but also from online citizen participation, we could make the case for implementing a new structure for governance at all levels of America. This would allow a more distributed method of harvesting innovation, as well as a way for citizens to participate more fully in our country's future.

I believe that Solutions Councils are an idea whose time has come. I see councils eventually stretching from the neighborhood level to the White House, each helping to harness the best innova-tions upon which a next era for America will be built.

PART FOUR

Building an Evolutionary Movement

In this final part, I want to address the deepest changes that I see as essential for us to fulfill our political potential and our spiritual destiny as a country in service to all. These changes in our operating system involve the building of a strategic, evolutionary political movement that aims for major long-term changes to our politics, our media, and our very systems for governing.

A new operating system for our country is not something that emerges overnight; it builds from values, ideas, and principles that are gradually woven into the structures of how we govern our country and relate to the rest of the world. I suspect that some of these changes may require more than several decades to even begin to implement. But by naming them and understanding why they are important for the long-term health and prosperity of our country, we can help ensure they are implemented when the timing is right. As I have shared, the America 7.0 operating system will build upon a sense of global consciousness and sacred citizenship. And it will take some time to fully emerge. In the end, though, it will result in systemic changes that translate into a truly peaceful, sustainable, healthy, and prosperous world.

So we begin our journey in this last part to become sacred citizens and better turn the wheels of our current democracy before then looking at the bigger question of how to build an enlightened political movement that can change our country and the world.

24

Sacred Citizenship

Citizenship is what makes a republic;
monarchies can get along without it.
—Mark Twain

ONE WAY TO THINK about how we catalyze the next evolution of our democracy is sacred citizenship—where we each choose to be conscious co-creators of a brighter future for America by marrying our deep wisdom with our constructive action. That's how we build America 7.0, step by step. Sacred citizenship is about grassroots political leadership that is undertaken in a spirit of oneness, respect, and love. It's about becoming an evolutionary who takes a global and local perspective at the same time. Sacred citizenship requires seeing our collective challenges from a deep, transpartisan perspective and then taking action in the service of real solutions. It is founded on being the change that we seek and aligning our lives with what serves the greatest good. A sacred citizen also approaches voting as a sacred commitment.

Let's begin with just two critical challenges for humanity where America has become a primary source of the problem and where sacred citizenship can become part of the solution. The first is global warming, one of the most insidious threats to humanity, with hundreds of millions of people in jeopardy as major ice shelves melt and climate changes alter weather patterns in devastating ways. America is the leading source per capita of the CO_2 that is driving global warming while our lifestyle is broadcast to the rest of the world, encouraging many others to copy it.

The stance of sacred citizenship would be to work supportively with politicians on lasting regulatory solutions *and* to take personal responsibility for being part of the solution ourselves. We might get solar for our roof, electric for our car, and offset the remainder of our carbon every month through a group such as *Carbonfund.org*, which effectively negates our contribution to global warming.

A second example, in the realm of facing international threats like terrorism from ISIS, is that a sacred citizen might recognize the danger of the polarization between America and Islam and work on a local solution, such as reaching out to Islamic members with a community potluck, or perhaps reaching out to build a bridge of relationship with an Islamic family in the Middle East to help shrink the divides.

These are only two major crises humanity as a whole is facing, and yet they are essential for us to face. Each crisis offers opportunities for engagement and strategic actions that may seem small but can translate into a major evolution of our country when multiplied over time. Each of us can make concrete, local steps to demonstrate positive, forward-moving citizenship in both realms. We can become our own climate change solution, our own emissary of reconciliation, and our own agent of innovation. We can blog and tweet our passions online and get involved going door to door for democratic reforms.

Sacred citizenship also means marrying our deep inner work with constructive, positive engagement with elected officials from the local to national levels. Our citizen leadership supports our elected leaders and holds them accountable by being in direct relationship. Sacred citizenship is all about creating a new generation of citizen leaders, ones who can embody new paradigms of living, foster innovative solutions, restore healthy democratic processes, and serve the planet rather than just self-interest. Each of us can become one of these leaders. Indeed, we really need *all* of us to become one.

Here's my recipe for how to become a sacred citizen leader who can help America choose an evolutionary path:

Invest in your personal growth—The first element of sacred citizenship is internal; our consciousness is the most important thing to change first. A sacred citizen becomes adept at working with the many tools for personal healing, conscious empowerment, and spiritual growth. Coaches, bodyworkers, therapists, priests, seminar leaders, and teachers can all be valuable allies on our path at different times. Utilizing these resources is part of becoming a clear and effective citizen leader, and it will allow us to guide others as well. As we do, we speak, write, and act from a deeper ground of being, one that ultimately brings people together.

Continue your education—Sacred citizenship requires us to understand the full breadth and depth of current problems. Today, this means keeping a finger on the pulse of new developments in everything from technology to politics. My recommendation is to read articles from the left and the right, as well as those that look at hidden truths. One innovative idea comes from transpartisan leader Michael Ostrolenk, who recommends a thirty-day fast from all our usual news sources and to just focus on news from sources that don't reflect our normal views. It's also helpful to get some information from the mainstream media while spending equal time investigating independent or overseas media sources, especially on the Internet. Alerting friends, neighbors, and allies to important information is a key activity of a sacred citizen.

Practice leadership—Look at every situation as an opportunity to practice leadership by example. This could be volunteering to run a church discussion group or a living room conversation, managing a team at work, or putting an end to child sex trafficking in your town. The challenges and problems of our leadership will manifest in whatever realm we lead. That's why it's good to have practice in more forgiving environments before taking on more substantial roles. If we don't work out the kinks in less consequential environments, we'll do so on a more public stage with larger consequences. While we grow in our leadership, it's also good to practice empowering others in their leadership, since great leaders are masterful at helping cultivate other leaders.

Spend time in both mainstream and alternative cultures—Mainstream culture tends to have more grounded systems of preparation and more effective skills trainings to develop expertise in leading organizations, companies, and systems. Alternative culture tends to have many visionary ideas and innovative solutions. Spending significant time engaging with people and media from both cultures is helpful preparation for sacred citizenship.

Mentor others—A key component of developing our leadership capacity is finding people we respect in our chosen domain and then establishing a mentor-mentee relationship. That may entail an apprenticeship, regular coaching, or simple friendship. Effective change leaders learn from other effective leaders and seek out those who can help them develop to the next level.

Walk your talk—If you are committed to sustainability, minimize your ecological footprint. If you believe in compassion for animals, become a vegetarian. If you believe in the importance of integrity, always tell the truth. Even the simple, quiet acts that no one will ever see have an effect on your leadership capacity. Those who do not walk their talk create barriers because their words are not authentic, real, or powerful. Integrity is a true leader's greatest source of power. I've always loved the story about Gandhi when a mother came and asked him to tell her son to stop eating sugar. Gandhi told her to come back in two weeks. She did and Gandhi then told her son, "Stop eating sugar!" When asked why the delay, he said, "Well, I had to stop eating sugar myself first."

Sacred citizenship requires us to be leaders through our presence and our actions. Our ability to grow into our clearest, highest, and most effective leadership—a process that takes time—will thus determine how helpful we can be to our country in the years ahead. Even if our acts now seem small and perhaps just involve our immediate community, they are empowering our journey to a better way of being together in this beautiful country and on this precious planet.

25

Turning the Wheels of Democracy

We must not, in trying to think about how we can make a big difference, ignore the small daily differences we can make which, over time, add up to big differences that we often cannot foresee.
—Marian Wright Edelman

THIS CHAPTER WILL FOCUS on a specific dimension of sacred citizenship, which is the power and importance of citizen lobbying. Even though I consider myself an engaged citizen and active participant in politics, until recently I had never visited one of our elected officials' offices. That's partially because something felt intimidating about it. The debates of Congress that do so much to shape our future always felt impenetrable—something that happens on CNN rather than something I can directly affect.

That changed in November 2014 when my wife and I attended the annual conference of the Friends Committee on National Legislation (FCNL), where 430 people (including more than 50 non-Quakers) from 41 states engaged in more than 200 visits to our members of Congress. We were fully equipped with training, talking points, and practice in how to become a citizen lobbyist in support of diplomacy with Iran as the best strategy to end its nuclear program and avert another war.

I was delighted by the welcome that our delegations received from smart and caring staff members in each of our congresspersons' offices. They were interested to hear our concerns and made it clear how seriously their bosses were taking the issue. They also helped us to understand nuances in the global diplomacy under way.

In Senator Barbara Boxer's office, more than twenty-five of us crowded into the conference room and shared our rehearsed case for asking her to reiterate her public support of the ongoing work of diplomacy with Iran. In Senator Dianne Feinstein's office, the twenty-four in our delegation made our case before being dazzled by the intelligence of her lead staff person's command of the subject. By the end of our time, we were all asking how we could better help him and Senator Feinstein. In a more intimate setting, with four of us visiting Representative Jared Huffman's staff, we had an engaging meeting in which they were very receptive to making a public statement. We came away feeling like we had started a longer-term relationship.

In all three visits, we drew upon powerful facts from the previous day's FCNL conference. For example, retired US Army Colonel Lawrence Wilkerson, a Republican who served as chief of staff under Secretary of State Powell, said that he had run scenario planning in previous administrations and they estimated a war with Iran would require five hundred thousand troops, ten years, and $1 trillion dollars, dwarfing both the Iraq and Afghanistan wars in terms of the impact to the United States and body counts, not to mention the provocative effect on terrorism.

I was surprised by how much we learned about geopolitics and the gears of democracy in our visits as the staff members shared, for instance, about the delicate dance with hardliners in Iran who had been firmly opposed to any détente.

Participating in this citizen lobbying led me to fully understand the rather obvious truth that our members of Congress are there to represent us. While I could say this objectively in the past,

I didn't really feel it on a visceral level. But there's nothing like direct personal experience to produce a shift.

At the end of the day, I came away deeply impressed that Quakers—who have only a hundred thousand or so active members—have had such a sustained impact on public policy by embracing political engagement as central to their faith. Their practical, non-polarizing advocacy has led to a long track record of effective citizen lobbying, building trust and respect on the Hill. As the largest peace lobby, they work both sides of the aisle to reduce military spending, promote diplomacy, prevent war, and champion social justice and sustainability. I also came away deeply impressed by the caliber of people who are called to serve our country by working in congressional offices: smart, dedicated, fully committed young leaders who work seventy-hour weeks in often intense circumstances to turn the wheels of democracy in a better direction.

Working within the halls of power requires a great deal of patience, as the wheels of democracy can turn painfully slowly. So FCNL's steadfast commitment and upbeat attitude were all the more admirable. We have since lobbied Representative Jared Huffman directly in his home office as well as written more regular letters on issues that matter, plus we returned to Washington in 2015 to lobby on behalf of the Atrocities Prevention Board.

Before FCNL, I had considered myself politically engaged because I would track the evening news and get involved in elections, mainly by backing candidates, throwing fundraisers, or writing columns online. What my direct experience with candidates made me realize, though, was that I was primarily focused on getting people elected who think like me rather than supporting those who have already won election and are now serving as government officials, regardless of their party or views. I realized that I was unconsciously feeding the problem rather than the solution.

As we've explored, one of the biggest challenges we now face is a political culture that is built on polarization. That culture is built and reinforced by the process of running for office. The nature of a political election requires that, at the end of the day, there is only one winner. That means a truly collaborative solution or outcome is not possible. The tendency, then, is for anyone who wants the job to become increasingly polarized against the other candidates and to build "teams" that wage verbal war against the other side to gain the prize of the elected position.

Once an electoral outcome is decided, though, a truly healthy democracy needs our representatives to clear the negative residue of the election in order to govern collaboratively. That's because effective governance requires a different skill set from running for office and, more importantly, a different culture. A highly polarized culture in which positions are seen as black or white is actually the opposite of what can lead to healthy compromises and synergistic solutions.

Part of creating a democracy that truly works is reducing the amount of competitive culture happening between elected officials so that solutions and agreements can be reached. This means containing the competitive, black-or-white culture of the electoral process so that it doesn't infect or overwhelm the synergistic, shades-of-gray, compromise-driven governance culture that we need.

With the injection of increasing amounts of money and longer political seasons, the result has been more polarized political parties. We then start thinking of politics as intrinsically debased because the overall culture becomes more about winning office and less about serving the governed. This isn't just a systemic problem. It's actually one that we are personally helping to create. When I thought of myself as being engaged in democracy because I was more active in the election cycle (and almost not at all in the governance cycle), I was actually unconsciously feeding the problem rather than the solution.

A more effective approach is to focus more energy into supporting the governance culture to be as wise as possible. Yes, we can and should be involved in elections; but if we do *less* of that than supporting the representatives who are already in place, we help the wheels of democracy turn as they were meant to turn.

If every week our political representatives heard from us about the things that matter to us *and* we were rewarding collaborative behavior rather than polarized stances outside of election cycles, we could help diminish and eventually transform our governance culture.

This shifts us from primarily seeing politics through the lens of trying to demand our own view triumphs to a process of working to optimize solutions and approaches among many constituents, viewpoints, and philosophies. It's really at the core of making democracy work anywhere.

The ability to take multiple viewpoints is a hallmark of maturity, and that is the precise capacity we most need for effective governance. If we are essentially building a more narcissistic, "my way or the highway" political culture, we reinforce the rigid viewpoints that lead to the breakdown in public trust.

I've learned a lot about this from watching the FCNL in action. They have a strong vision and agenda for peace and will talk with anyone and work with whoever is in power to advance key pieces of legislation. They demonstrate for us that there is always the opportunity to find common ground and work respectfully. They've done this for seventy-five years now and are respected by both Democrats and Republicans, which has opened the door to a truly supportive and respectful role in the machinery of our national politics.

While FCNL is doing great work to advocate for specific policies and positions, their more general modeling may be even more important. They show that getting involved in collaborative and respectful citizen lobbying with elected officials is ultimately more effective in creating real change than simply backing another candidate for office who mirrors our views.

Toward a Strategic Political Movement

If there was one decision I would overrule, it would be Citizens United. I think the notion that we have all the democracy that money can buy strays so far from what our democracy is supposed to be.
—Ruth Bader Ginsburg

FEW PEOPLE WOULD ARGUE that our current political process is balanced and fair. Big money and special interests skew the decision-making of both major parties. Third parties that are focused on fundamental reforms of the system may play the role of spoilers when they attempt to draw voters away from the major parties. The way the political game is constructed, the best we can often do is to put our energy behind the party that we believe will do a moderately better job. This approach, though, makes it challenging to create a major upgrade of the whole paradigm of politics. Neither major party has an interest in seeing the nature of the political process change in a way that threatens its base of influence. Each electoral season, reform-oriented groups tend to end up voting within the duopoly out of fear of how dire the situation will be if the other party assumes power. Thus we remain in the Democratic-Republican tug-of-war, which doesn't always allow for more significant forms of collective evolution.

Alternatively, if we become an Independent or third-party voter, we may undermine our goals in the short term by helping the other political wing, as happened with progressives who supported Nader in 2000. What can we do as concerned citizens who know something much better is possible for America?

Part of the answer is forging a strategic political movement designed to create the kind of long-term, systemic changes required for a true upgrade to the American operating system that we've been discussing in this book. Many of these changes will take a long time and a lot of patience. They cut to the core of how decisions are made and how power is wielded. Such a movement is a bit more like playing chess than protesting in the streets to demand change now, as important as those actions are. For long-term success, good strategy is a necessity.

Most people don't know that Rosa Parks's famed bus protest in Montgomery was part of a much larger strategy for the civil rights movement. She had trained at the Highlander Folk School for nonviolent change only months before her protest galvanized the movement. Her protest was thus not spontaneous but part of a larger strategy for the civil rights movement.

For those who want real evolution of the United States' political system, we need to become better at this kind of long-term strategy or we will be relegated to the sidelines, either voicing critiques of the "system" or waxing poetic about idealistic visions of the future without having any real impact on power dynamics today.

Developing a strategic approach to major political change requires a number of things. First, we've got to be willing to believe that major upgrades are possible. If we believe our current system is unfixable, it saps our energy and creativity from finding the evolutionary path forward. Instead, we can view the most serious problems as opportunities—each is a pain point that can help galvanize people to work together on creating a larger shift.

After we've opened ourselves to expanded possibilities, the next step is gathering leaders or potential leaders who share enough of a vision of what an evolution of our political system will look like—perhaps including goals such as a commitment to sustainability, clean money elections, global alliances, etc. When these leaders can find enough common ground—a vision of the most essential reforms required to create the next "blueprint"—then we can create a political movement guided by strategy.

Given the Democratic and Republican reins on power and the nature of the "spoiler effect" without instant runoff voting, a precondition for such a new movement is that it cannot be located solely within either political party or exist separately as a third party that runs its own candidates. In the next chapter I will explore an "enlightened wings" approach that charts a path to a higher possibility within each party, but ultimately this evolutionary political movement can't be constrained by party ideology. It will need to emerge as a political force that is committed to creating a new paradigm while also being willing to work with leaders across the spectrum, both inside and outside parties.

The shared political movement might simply be called "Evolutionary Politics" or another name that emerges organically. In 2016, a group that has formed under the banner of transpartisan politics is convening an online American Citizens Summit in partnership with The Shift Network that will have online and live components and will look at policies and movement building that go beyond conventional lines. This summit holds great promise as a watershed moment for building a more strategic, transpartisan approach to evolving our democracy.

Serving as an antidote to the power of special-interest lobbies, this evolutionary political movement will need to resemble a collective-interest group that is willing, just like more narrow special-interest groups, to cast support behind political leaders who are willing to collaborate to advance a blueprint for a new society. One of the most interesting sources for thinking about how to create such an evolutionary, transpartisan political movement comes from the Institute for Cultural Evolution, created by Steve McIntosh and Carter Phipps. They have done an excellent job of applying integral theory to practical political issues and movement building.

An evolutionary political movement informed by sacred principles can become an influential lever to gain commitments to major reform planks from both sides of the aisle in DC. In order to do this, though, a political movement will eventually require an infrastructure, including media, organizing groups, technical infrastructure, PR expertise, organizers, strategists, fundraising mechanisms, and coordinated actions. It will also require a sizable base of support.

If such a political force gains the support of even a small percent of the US population and uses that base effectively, it could act as a tipping point force in elections locally and nationally. On the left, Greens have tried to act as more of this force and on the right, Libertarians, although the challenge is that they are both wedded to one side of the aisle. The key is to have an organizing base of interest that is not solely dependent upon or beholden to either major party but can exert leverage within both.

The goal is to create infrastructure for an evolutionary movement that works with Democrats, Republicans, and potentially third parties to affect more fundamental reforms and evolution. This movement need not be oppositional; it can be a great ally to political leaders. An independent, grassroots infrastructure that can be mobilized around key legislative advances can help a president or governor make bolder moves forward. Women's suffrage and the civil rights movement both represented organized movements outside the political system that had a profound effect on political processes.

One important note here, surfaced by transpartisan pioneer John Steiner, is that such a strategic political movement should be careful to differentiate between the *content*—such as specific political reforms—and the *process* for getting to those reforms. Many change movements have been spearheaded solely to get a certain piece of legislation passed, but there's an equally important (or perhaps even more important) function, which is to design more effective collaborative processes. The Bridge Alliance, for instance, is a transpartisan initiative that focuses on creating synergy between different groups that are already focused on a particular set of agendas. So there's an important function for holding a container for collaboration and not just identifying with specific planks or policies to move forward.

Another example that holds some promise for being an evolutionary political movement is the Network of Spiritual Progressives (NSP), founded by Rabbi Michael Lerner of *Tikkun*. Its founding vision champions specific, far-ranging policies that reflect a 7.0 worldview and a particularly powerful vision of a Global Marshall Plan that proposes dedicating 1 to 2 percent of the United States' annual GDP each year for the next twenty years to eliminate domestic and global poverty, homelessness, hunger, inadequate education, and inadequate health care and repair environmental damage. While it's not clear if NSP will ultimately gain sufficient momentum and traction, the impulse is in the right direction, marrying a higher perspective on the political process with a specific set of policies that is independent of party identity. However, like the Greens, it tends to focus mainly on the Democrat side rather than working on both sides of the political divide, such as groups like the FCNL do.

On the right, there are exciting developments happening with leaders who also see the need for an evolution in consciousness. The Institute for Cultural Evolution launched the Project for the Future Right, a group that had a productive first summit at the ranch of Whole Foods CEO John Mackey in 2015 and a second gathering in the summer of 2016, including several members of

Congress. Richard Tafel, a founder of the Log Cabin Republicans and director of this new initiative, commented to me that the Future Right draws upon a combination of both libertarian and conservative principles with an eye toward building an inclusive, right-leaning tent. Three core pillars emerged from the first conclave: a respect for individual freedom, respect for the power of conscious capitalism, and commitment to religious liberty. Participants in this effort also share a commitment to transpartisan collaboration rather than hyperpartisan gridlock.

Because the cultural and political warfare between Democrats and Republicans has gotten so intense over the last years, it can be quite hard to attempt to build alliances and momentum on both sides. The nature of warfare often forces a choosing of sides. However, when we succumb to that polarization and start identifying solely with one side or the other, we end up exaggerating the divide rather than transforming it. The truth is that for America to go to the next level, it's going to take major changes on both sides of the aisle. The most powerful reforms will ultimately need to be embraced by both major parties, often for different motives such as those we explored in discussing a higher minimum wage or reducing incarceration rates.

One of the low-hanging fruits for transpartisan collaboration should be real campaign finance reform through a 28th Constitutional Amendment, an issue that is very popular on both the left and right. That's because so long as big money is distorting our democracy, it's virtually impossible to do major upgrades to the laws or processes that govern our land, much less open the door to outstanding political candidates who are not wealthy.

The distorting effects of money on our democracy are extreme: to put some numbers on it, according to Mark Gerzon's book *The Reunited States of America*, one quarter of 1 percent of our citizens give more than two-thirds of the campaign contributions to candidates, which means there are very strong incentives to listen to deep-pocketed elites. A smaller and smaller group of citizens is having an outsize effect on our laws. Furthermore, according to the Democratic Congressional Campaign Committee, candidates now spend four hours every day calling big donors for money, which effectively hamstrings them from studying issues in depth and focusing their time on making wise decisions on pending legislation.[1] So not only do we have our democracy shaped by fewer people, our political leaders spend less and less of their time doing what we elected them to do. This also makes it harder than ever for non-wealthy candidates to mount a credible campaign.

The good news is that getting big money out of politics through a constitutional amendment is something that is fairly achievable in the coming years, especially since major political candidates such as Hillary Clinton are already supportive and a very high percentage of Americans agree that excessive money in politics is an issue that needs to be fixed.

Cenk Uygur, the founder of Wolf PAC, which is one of the key groups leading the charge on an amendment to get money out of politics, makes the point that virtually every generation of Americans has gotten one constitutional amendment (or more) passed. The Constitution explicitly planned for these upgrades to be possible from a state level so that if things become too corrupt in Washington itself, two-thirds of the states can get together and call for a Constitutional Convention on a specific issue. In 2014, Vermont became the first state to call for a 28th Constitutional Amendment for Free and Fair Elections, and there are currently many other initiatives in other states en route. Wolf PAC is focused on building this movement state by state, while other groups are more focused on lobbying Congress directly for the change. In addition to being essential to reform our democracy and free our legislators to do their job well, a constitutional amendment to get the big money out of politics will also build our confidence in our ability to create deeper systemic change.

Another area that should become a focus for this strategic political movement is the issue of congressional districting, which has dramatically worsened the problem of political polarization by creating more and more districts that are noncompetitive. In 1992, there were 103 swing districts—those that had a margin of victory in the presidential race of less than five percentage points—but by 2012, only 35 swing districts remained.[2] As more and more districts become less competitive, it tends to exaggerate the polarization of politics because the main competition for each seat tends to come from the same party, which pushes candidates ever further to an extreme. Over time, partisan redistricting has diminished political leaders' motivation to collaborate with the other party or to offer moderate positions because their main political challenges come from the more extreme factions within their own party.

A related issue is how elections are adjudicated by the Federal Election Commission, which currently consists of three Democrats and three Republicans. With four votes required to move changes forward, the body is effectively frozen in its ability to make any major changes. Shifting the representation on this board so that all the seats are held by respected, neutral, transpartisan representatives would also go a long way toward ensuring the kind of unbiased oversight that leads to real fairness.

In the next chapter, we'll look more at how to build a movement that works with both major parties on substantive changes like these.

27

Transcending Political Polarities

The American spirit wears no political label. In service to others and yes, in sacrifice for our country, there are no Republicans; there are no Democrats; there are only Americans.
—Senator John Kerry

AMERICA'S POLITICAL LANDSCAPE HAS evolved for quite some time as a duopoly of power, which can make change outside of the system seem almost possible to create. Democrats and Republicans hold nearly all substantial political positions in our country and together set our nation's course. Their rivalry for supremacy creates and reinforces a strong polarity in the American psyche and tends to reduce options to the positions that these two parties articulate. To the extent that their core ideas or positions are inadequate, America's ability to chart a wise path is compromised. Also, both parties have a vested interest in protecting the duopoly on power rather than allowing other perspectives and players into the game.

It's a tricky situation and not at all easy to see the pathway forward.

I do think a more enlightened path is possible, though. We begin with the fundamental principle of enlightenment, which is that it transcends and includes dualities. A more enlightened political process must therefore transcend but include this duopoly in some significant ways. Those who seek reform of the two major parties and want to open the door to deeper political reforms tend to split into two camps: insiders and outsiders. Insiders consider themselves realists and advocate for working within a major party. Third party "spoiler" effects, they say, make working outside the system potentially dangerous because it splits votes on their wing and gives more power to the other wing.

The outsiders tend to believe that the major parties are beholden to special interests and that no meaningful reform is possible from within. If we allow ourselves to be corralled into one of the two major parties, they believe, our voice will largely be irrelevant. The only way to shake the system out of its stagnation is by working from the outside.

I believe there is another strategy that has the long-term potential to evolve politics toward its next higher level of expression. This strategy starts with respect for the power of a polarity to advance evolution. The polarization into masculine and feminine sexes has clear evolutionary advantages, for example. There's a positive evolutionary tension that comes from that polarity—a reshuffling of genes, a specialization into roles, a complementary synergy. If this kind of polarization did not have value, it would not have endured over millions of years of evolution.

In the political realm, humans are generally wired to orient around two primary political leanings, one that is more conservative and the other more progressive. Instead of erasing that dichotomy, or even trying to blend them, the most evolutionary stance is to encourage each political impulse to find its highest and most enlightened expression. If we adopt such an approach, the task is not to convert people who are naturally disposed to the other pole, but to encourage each pole's more evolved expression and then to harmonize those two poles to work together more effectively.

This recognition is also at the heart of transpartisanship, which doesn't seek to erase our differences but rather find a higher ground to engage differences constructively. Jim Turner, who worked with Ralph Nader and coauthored *Voice of the People*, argues that the better the partisan, the better the transpartisan—so long as the transpartisan comes to the table with an open mind and an open heart. It's thus not about abandoning our convictions but rather finding ways to engage from a higher level and encourage both parties to mature.

We can think about this as a series of stages through which people with different political inclinations pass, from more egocentric (What's in it for me?) to socio-centric (What's best for my community?) to world-centric (What's best for the world?). At each stage of development the political polarity remains, but the context is increasingly one of concern for a larger whole. So how do we get more Democrats and Republicans to operate from a world-centric level—the global consciousness we've been discussing at the foundation of America 7.0?

What I'm suggesting on a practical level is the development of an enclave or caucus within the Democratic Party that embodies the next, higher, global, transpartisan expression of the progressive mind-set. This group would run its own candidates for Democratic primaries. If its candidates were to win the primary, they would then become the Democratic nominees. It not, they would put their support behind the Democrat who did. This avoids some of the third-party spoiler effects.

Such a group's ultimate aim would be to evolve the Democratic Party itself through candidates who offer more enlightened and transpartisan principles. However, it would respect that such an evolution would take time. In the meantime, the group would back those candidates that most closely mirror its positions, while building a base of power within the party.

This approach would then be paired with and engaged in active collaboration with a more enlightened expression of the conservative impulse, which would also run its own candidates and platforms for Republican primaries.

Over time, a more evolved wing would grow in both parties, by both attracting new people and helping committed partisans to open to new possibilities, until our collective evolution allows us to directly elect the candidates who represent this next level of more conscious politics. When that happens, the polarity of parties will be seen more synergistically; we will recognize that the "opposing" values are necessary and complementary.

The names that come to me to describe the next-level versions of both parties are the Evolutionary Democrats and the Evolutionary Republicans. Even while many of my allies argue for using "transpartisan," what I like about the term "evolutionary" is that it signifies that the worldview of both would be about pioneering new possibilities for our country and that there is not a final, fixed destination. It's a process of growing still further and making a conscious separation from our revolutionary past. As explored in Part One, evolutionaries carry a more patient and respectful spirit than revolutionaries, with less bombast and more collaboration.

Both wings of evolutionaries would maintain a deep respect for alternative political positions and think in a more integrative fashion about the evolution of the whole. The Evolutionary Democrats would likely emphasize the healthy design of supportive social systems to advance society. On the other side of the aisle, Evolutionary Republicans would be advocates for growth with an emphasis on the personal accountability and business side of the equation.

Both emergent wings would thus have continuity with the past, as well as represent a higher octave of expression. The combined naming of an evolutionary political movement would speak to the higher-order synthesis that can emerge as we recognize our complementarity. People would have "dual identity," in that part of their identity is with their chosen party and part is with the group of evolutionaries from the other party as well. This respects that we have individual differences in temperament while still reaching toward higher ground.

There could be large conferences or gatherings that feature leaders from both party wings, which would start to break down the social separation that reinforces partisan warfare.

With this "more enlightened enclave" strategy, people from across the political spectrum who share the recognition that our political life needs to evolve to the next level would have a way to champion more enlightened values by running primary candidates while also building a long-term power base to assume actual leadership roles whenever a sufficient number of voters agree with their perspective. On both sides of the aisle, we would be laying the groundwork for a higher-level reunion in which our polarized identities are softened, battle lines are erased, and our righteous positioning is recognized as partial.

In the next chapter, I'll look more at what a more enlightened left and right can look like, but it's an important first step for each of us to recognize that there *is* a more enlightened octave of each party and to support its emergence patiently.

28

A More Enlightened Left *and* Right

Personal transformation can and does have global effects. As we go,
so goes the world, for the world is us. The revolution that will save
the world is ultimately a personal one.
—Marianne Williamson

BUILDING UPON THE IDEAS in the last chapter, it becomes clear
that for America to evolve to the next level, whichever party is in
power must do its best to demonstrate a higher, more enlightened
path forward. If the party succeeds, it becomes more magnetic
to voters and thus more compelling to reelect. If it does not succeed but instead delivers business-as-usual politics, the pendulum
can swing back the other way. The task for the party that is out of
power then becomes to forge a more comprehensive platform itself
so that when the pendulum swings back, it does not just result in
the horizontal transfer of power from left to right but also verti-
cally to another level of consciousness, thereby withdrawing power
from less evolved positions in both parties.

Those in power often make the mistake of orienting around
retaining power by undermining/combatting the other rather than
putting their full intelligence into demonstrating greater wisdom
with the power they have already been given. Putting the focus on
demonstrating great maturity and mastery eventually forces the rival

political party to find its own higher ground. As both Republicans and Democrats find their higher octave of expression, we can have a political process with more wisdom, integrity, and depth, which in turn can help America reach its full potential.

The next step on that journey for those who lean to the left is to create a more enlightened, transpartisan enclave within the Democratic Party, which I have called the Evolutionary Democrats for the sake of argument, with a vision for our future that is bold, beautiful, and compelling. This enclave needs to paint the picture of a sustainable, healthy, and just world with visionary power and then deliver compelling strategies, policies, and activities that can achieve that vision. Influencing a single presidency is not enough—it requires a full vision that candidates at multiple levels can embrace over the long term, covering levels from the local to the global.

Once fully articulated, that vision requires integrity and boldness to translate into concrete policies and actions. Then citizens can't help but be drawn to continue the movement forward. For the Democratic Party as a whole to find its next level of expression, it means getting people excited by this next order vision.

Following are some essential elements of that wholeness that I think will need to be included for Evolutionary Democrats to demonstrate a more enlightened version of the progressive impulse:

> *Spirituality*—Over the last decades, much of the soul has been drained from the Democratic Party by making too strong a separation from spirituality. Spirituality can be a great unifier, especially when it fully embraces all religions as well as non-religious spiritual expression. Evolutionary Democrats would be well served to transcend some of their ambivalence about the spiritual needs of humans and address them with a more inclusive stance.

Love—The impulse behind progressivism is more connected to the Nurturant Parent model, according to cognitive linguist George Lakoff, which is in turn a reflection of love.[1] However, the actual feeling and even the words of love are often absent from much of the Democratic Party's discourse, which leads to a lack of alignment between the intention (caring for the greatest number of citizens) and the presentation (which tends to emphasize rational self-interest of lower and middle classes).

A healthy respect for hierarchy—Democrats often rebel against hierarchy and overemphasize equality, which has sometimes led to disorganized movements and fractious internal politics. Organizational excellence requires a balance between hierarchy of skill and equality of being. Democrats as a whole need more respect for mastery (which is a reflection of hierarchy of skill) so that progressive organizations can achieve more excellence.

Financial mastery—Democrats are sometimes prone to think of money as a necessary evil rather than an engine for the good. The simple truth is that when more money flows to more good-hearted individuals, our society benefits, since these individuals can steward these resources in wise ways. On the simplest level, money is a vehicle for expressing our values. The left's tendency to rail against wealth doesn't really serve. Neither does a more cynical corporate "realism." Evolutionary Democrats need to become more masterful at making money and guiding it wisely.

Integrating the warrior—Democrats have often dissociated from the warrior side, assuming that aggressive impulses are intrinsically bad. However, that sometimes leads voters, many of whom are quite fearful of threats such as crime and terrorism, to have greater trust in more muscular Republicans. A more enlightened left will not dissociate from the warrior energy but harness it in the service of something higher. A sacred warrior does not avoid taking a strong stand for truth and justice because of fear of the public's perception.

Personal responsibility—A core value on the Republican side of the equation that needs greater integration on the left is the principle of personal responsibility. The tendency to put blame on systems for societal problems can create a culture of victims unable and unwilling to take responsibility for their actions and for their future. A more balanced understanding requires us to acknowledge both the truth of societal responsibility *and* the truth of personal responsibility. Both are essential to create real solutions.

Relating well to the right—Evolutionary Democrats can bracket politics and have meaningful, deep relationships with those on the other side of the political polarity— from friendship to teamwork all the way to getting married. This is essential to create the transpartisan ground of collaboration.

Fun—Evolutionary Democrats need to learn how to be more fun. The more reactionary forces on the right tend to prey on fear, creating a stiff, serious, and oppressive mood. The antidote is being more colorful and light, which is more magnetic. Comedians such as Jon Stewart and Stephen Colbert use humor masterfully to illuminate the truth of current political realities while also holding that truth lightly. Building fun into the political process makes it "stickier" and more likely to encourage ongoing engagement.

The Evolutionary Democrats who embody this kind of integration are often reluctant to run for office. They may see running for office as overly ambitious and self-interested. Some of the most respected left-leaning leaders tend to run nonprofits. Running a government is similar to running a nonprofit—the core challenge involves mobilizing people behind a vision for our collective good and then successfully executing a game plan for how to do so.

Evolutionary Democrats would be wise to recruit some of the most respected and successful nonprofit leaders who have the leadership skills necessary to both govern and mobilize citizens behind a shared vision. Some may not want to run, which is all the more reason to convince them to do so. Leaders with nonprofit credibility will likely not govern out of self-interest to the same degree and will more likely embody the full-spectrum approach to politics about which I'm writing.

A more evolutionary enclave of the Democratic Party will also come up with innovative policy ideas and solutions that integrate traditional right-wing values. For example, we might see policies that lead to such things as an American Microlending Program, in which the federal government matches the investments of individuals in inner city small businesses to help lift people out of poverty *and* make a return on investment. Or a Federal Green Venture Fund that takes billions of federal dollars and co-invests it in clean tech alongside top VC firms, just as university endowments do. With such a fund, instead of spending tax dollars with no return, we could make profitable clean-tech investments that generate good American jobs *and* fund social programs, which would allow taxes to decrease. Such a path combines personal responsibility and entrepreneurism with creating a strong social net—a both/ and approach. More important than the actual policies and programs that would be created by a more enlightened left would be an enhanced respect for balanced collaboration and solutions.

This overall strategy begins to bring an "elder" wing into the Democratic Party, including those with clarity and wisdom more directly in the political process and advising those who are now the mainstream of Democratic politicians. Eventually I see this group articulating a higher-order platform for Evolutionary Democrats that is also grounded in a sacred worldview, thus acting as a new center of gravity that can pull more conventional candidates toward it. In this way, we can patiently evolve a new and more effective operating system for the Democratic Party as a whole, one that is aligned with deeper wisdom.

On the other side of the aisle, the creation of a more enlightened right goes hand in hand with the creation of a more enlightened left. As happens in any relationship, when one side of a polarity experiences growth, it can help accelerate growth in the other. A more enlightened left automatically encourages a more enlightened right (and vice versa) since they will need to keep pace with their rivals for votes, money, and attention.

When I say "enlightened right," some on the left cringe—they believe that enlightened values, principles, and ideals are found entirely on the left. However, that vantage doesn't see the situation deeply enough. There are noble, beautiful, deep, generous, caring, wise, skilled, and dynamic people on the right, just as there are on the left. The difference is one of personal predilection— where do we naturally gravitate?

Instead of judging one side of the political polarity as intrinsically better, it is wiser to respect each as the expression of a sacred impulse. We each have our rightful role to play here, and we're better off encouraging the best in each other rather than condemning the traits we don't share.

So although I'm a transpartisan progressive, I do find it valuable to reflect on what a more enlightened right looks like, bearing in mind that groups such as the Future Right are likely going to create their own more authentic vision. Here are a few principles:

Progress-oriented conservatism—Has a deep respect and love for the past and for what we've already achieved without that love turning into a resistance to the process of change. Believes in progress that is pragmatic and that builds upon the past in respectful ways.

Entrepreneurial with checks and balances—Celebrates the power of free enterprise while recognizing that it needs to take place in a context that has checks and balances on power, including healthy laws and market regulation. Sees government's job as creating a healthy business climate that encourages dynamic free enterprise by setting a fair and level playing field with protections against harm.

Inner-disciplined—Does not believe that problems are solved simply by allocating more money but through developing internal capacity in parallel with outer opportunities. Emphasis on moral development, self-reliance, and education.

Green—Embraces the virtue of sustainability because it results in greater financial well-being, improved conservation of natural resources, and enhanced national security, as well as leaving a healthier planet as a legacy for our grandchildren.

Global—Recognizes that we live in a global economy and that to perform well we need to think and act with a global orientation, as global citizens. Cares about the well-being of people from other countries and nations. Sees enhanced trade as a path to mutual benefit, not just unilateral gain. Encourages entrepreneurism in other countries rather than classical aid.

Pro-liberties—Believes in personal liberties and the freedom to make choices. Does not legislate morality, even while striving to live from a high level of personal morality and integrity. Strong supporter of freedom of expression and religion, as well as championing the rights of underdogs and traditionally marginalized groups.

Wisdom-seeker—Remains open to the wisdom of all religious traditions and all people. Culls wisdom from his or her own tradition while respecting the wisdom of others. Has a growth-oriented inner life.

Open to science—Embraces the inquiry of science as well as its conclusions even when those contradict traditional religious teachings.

Humorous—Has the ability to not take life too seriously, takes great enjoyment in living and laughing.

Relates well to the left—Can bracket politics and have meaningful, deep relationships with those on the other side of the political aisle, from friendship to teamwork all the way to getting married—a strong transpartisan foundation.

This is not, of course, a list of requirements. But it does start to paint the broad brushstrokes of a more enlightened right that is emerging, that will be further articulated by groups such as Future

Right.. This more enlightened right serves as an improvement over the reactionary factions of the Republican Party that have contributed to a frozen and polarized political landscape.

Evolutionary Republicans are committed to progress—economic, moral, scientific—as well as personal growth and maturity. As the Tea Party begins to wane in influence, it's a ripe moment to consciously assemble a more evolutionary and transpartisan wing of the Republican Party that can energize the party with ideas that appeal to a broader base. The Tea Party has, in many ways, become the embodiment of the revolutionary impulse in the party—impatient, demanding, rebellious, taking its name and identity from the American Revolutionaries who threw British tea into Boston Harbor. As shared in a previous chapter, this isn't the spirit that will lead us to the next level of our maturation as a country. There are many worthwhile positions in the Tea Party, but if the spirit is one of disrespecting viewpoints that are not one's own and forcing one's ideology on others, it will eventually flame out as a movement because it isn't offering a sufficiently positive and constructive vision of what we are moving toward to enroll the bulk of Americans. It will become the hideout for those who are stuck in rigid and revolutionary identities.

In order to have integrated, sustainable progress as a country, we need to evolve on all levels and with as many people as possible. The virtues, disciplines, and skills offered by Evolutionary Republicans will prove just as valuable as the virtues, disciplines, and skills offered by Evolutionary Democrats. As these two more enlightened groups emerge in parallel (or groups with different names but similar transpartisan intent), they can demonstrate a shared commitment to cultural growth while respecting their differences.

29

Training Future Political Leaders

*Great men are they who see that spiritual is stronger than any
material force, that thoughts rule the world.*
—Ralph Waldo Emerson

POLITICS IS ONE OF the few high-profile career occupations in
which on-the-job training is the norm. The election process itself
also requires quite different skills from those required for effective
governance, which means we often elect great campaigners rather
than great governors. The ability to triumph over an opposing
candidate does not necessarily lend itself to skilled and thoughtful
policies built in collaboration with other leaders.

Politics may well require the greatest range of skills of any career
in our society: knowledge of complex systems, laws, and regulation;
fundraising talent; skilled speechmaking; a broad understanding of
our society; well-honed judgment; the ability to run large operations;
and the emotional intelligence to work with a wide range of people
and constituencies. Law school has often been the training ground
for political leaders, and it indeed offers effective training for the
lawmaking function of politics. However, politics is ultimately
as much about leadership as it is about lawmaking, as much about
ethics as speechmaking. Judging from the number of scandals that
beset elected officials, the personal development side of leadership

is something we are not adequately preparing these leaders for in today's America.

In the next evolution of America, I believe we will start to groom our future political leaders with far more care. The quality of their consciousness and the depth of their integrity have a massive impact on our society. In a more evolved society, we cannot have political leaders who are unconsciously acting out their shadows, reinforcing regressive behaviors, creating polarized games, or doing corrupt backroom deals. We need political leaders who are clear-thinking, wise, healthy, and whole, with strong skills to operate effectively as leaders. Simply put, to build a more sacred America we need more conscious political leaders.

Leadership skills are learnable. A combination of deep personal work, self-development practices, coaching, training, and ongoing mentoring can help political leaders ensure that their leadership is outstanding. Harnessing the most sophisticated tools we have available may include clearing patterns from the past, understanding interpersonal dynamics, and developing skills at managing complex organizations. These are the skills that executive coaches are paid to work on with senior leaders, which is considered a vital investment by many companies. While bad business leaders can run a company into the ground, a dysfunctional political leader can damage our whole society. So this type of coaching and support is even more imperative in the political sphere.

I thus believe that as we evolve the next level of our country we will need to develop more sophisticated programs for training future political leaders, especially early in their adult lives. These programs will not only provide them with campaign organizing skills or the know-how to pass laws but also act as leadership development programs that help them cultivate greater virtue, develop better team-building skills, and become more wise.

The careful training of political leaders might begin in their late twenties or thirties, after their careers have started to form and their leanings toward political service are evident. After a decade or more in the world of work, they will have already developed sufficient self-awareness to enter into a process of maturation and leadership training. Every aspect of political leadership could be offered in its best-in-class form, from speech training to management skills to coalition building.

Such a training would provide the internal "software" necessary to become a more enlightened political leader. Ideally, such a training would include Republicans, Democrats, and Independents so that it is not a training in political position but in developing effective political leaders. By mixing the full spectrum of political positions in a political training program, we would also help participants to go beyond partisanship and work more collaboratively once in office. To build upon the ideas in previous chapters, we might call this the Evolutionary Politics Leadership Academy, and it would specifically not be about party affiliation but about the hard and soft skills necessary for effective leadership for those who aspire to serve in the political sphere. By working with potential political leaders over multiple years, we would go a long way toward cultivating a next level of wisdom in our political process, especially if that training were considered a real value-add in the minds of parties and voters.

Given the intense pressures once a political candidacy is declared, it will be more effective to encourage the personal growth to happen well in advance. Our deepest self grows in a slower fashion than can be accommodated in fast-paced campaigns. Plus, on-the-job mistakes can be costly to society. Establishing habits of meditation, self-reflection, and inner development at a younger age would strengthen a candidate's inner development and generate resiliency that could be drawn upon in office.

One model template for a future political leadership program is the Emerge America program that trains Democratic women leaders, which now has chapters in fourteen states.[1] They give women leaders who are considering running for office a comprehensive program of skills trainings. They also offer a strong ongoing community of support that helps women candidates overcome other barriers. This program has the dual benefit of encouraging more women to run for office as well.

In the military, we have academies that train the officers of tomorrow in the leadership skills they will need. An Evolutionary Politics Leadership Academy would be a powerful parallel, built on sacred and transpartisan principles. It would groom women and men to be great leaders exemplifying the highest integrity and best leadership skills. Such an investment in our nation's future would pay incredible dividends in the long term, especially when that training is seen as a prerequisite for service in national office. Potential leaders would be able to use the time of preparation to work out psychological shadows, develop inner fortitude, and train in the leadership skills that will be sorely needed in the future, as well as discern if they are in fact suited for the job. This kind of investment in training would better prepare candidates for the unique pressures and potentials inherent in elected office and empower graduates to be inspiring and effective servants of the public good.

30

The Shift Network

When I look into the future, it's so bright it burns my eyes.
—Oprah Winfrey

IN THIS CHAPTER, I will share more about The Shift Network's vision and how it can help evolve America and our world. One of the most important tasks ahead of us is to empower and unify the grassroots leaders who are meant to lead the next evolution of our country (and world) and give them the inspiration, tools, and teachings that will allow them to give their greatest gifts.

I first received a vision for such a network in the year 2000 during a meditation retreat. For nearly three days, a detailed roadmap came to me of a global education and media network that would empower conscious leaders, spread the latest innovations, enlighten and educate people, and offer templates for the new culture. It was clear to me that this network would act as an accelerator of personal and collective evolution and become a major force for the good. It was both dazzling and daunting.

I assumed that because the vision was so compelling and the need so apparent, it would be relatively easy to manifest. I was very naive. After spending a year on attempting to launch it without success (and running up $65,000 in credit card debt), I had to think again. I needed more skills, networks, and time to develop as a leader. So after grieving the first failure, I spent some years work-ing as a marketing consultant before I was given a second chance under the banner of the Institute of Noetic Sciences, a nonprofit research institute. Over four years, I grew the Shift in Action pro-gram to 10,000 paying members globally, with free media that had been watched by a million people and grossed annual revenues over $1 million. However, the board decided it no longer wanted to continue that direction, so I reluctantly came to the conclusion it was time to let it all go.

Releasing this second attempt proved to be a blessing in dis-guise, because the third version of this global network—started ten years after the first—has become a rapidly growing and profitable success, with more than 700,000 people having participated in one of our free offerings and customers in 150 countries. We have a dedicated team of fifty people who work alongside more than fifty faculty who teach transformational courses and trainings in every-thing from spiritual growth to peacebuilding to conscious business to holistic health to shamanism. Our plan is to grow an online Shift University that offers training in the evolutionary skills needed to lead this next evolution of our world. In addition, we have featured over one thousand conscious-change leaders in our free summits in areas from holistic health to sustainability to peace to parenting.

In the next phase, we plan to grow The Shift Network's conscious-change platform with a Shift Media group and our own online Shift TV that chronicles the positive stories of how people are co-creating the new culture in exciting local ways. This is important because shifting the media is central to evolving America. The average American watches television a staggering four hours every day. The Internet consumes a growing slice of our attention, and adding drive-time radio, magazines, newspa-pers, podcasts, Internet video, and movies means we are constantly swimming in media.

This stream of media sculpts our consciousness and our perspective on the world, as well as our values, beliefs, and principles. It powerfully affects what we buy and how we think. It can galvanize us into collective action, spur social outrage, or sway the outcome of elections. On the positive side, media can offer human society new models for how to live, heal social wounds, and advance real solutions.

The vast majority of our media, however, reinforces the worldview we're outgrowing. It tends to be polarizing, consumer-driven, mind-deadening, and violence-saturated. We see the horrors of humanity regularly, the great breakthroughs more rarely. It often acts as a narcotic rather than an awakening force. Even alternative media tends to be more polarizing than positive, evolutionary, and sacred. Our media will thus need to evolve in substantial ways in the next America to fully emerge.

Now imagine that we had a more enlightened media network and its primary job was to offer positive solutions, thoughtful perspectives, and inspiring examples of what is working to move us toward a better world. What if every morning we received innovative ideas in bite-sized packages on our smartphone? What if we received a weekly magazine with the most important new breakthroughs in our global culture as well as methods for us to replicate those breakthroughs in our own communities?

At The Shift Network, we are in the process of envisioning and developing such a global media network that is focused on real solutions and evolutionary perspectives. Our goal is to create a cross-platform media brand that delivers content that is awakening, healing, and transformative. Shift Media will reflect the same values that I've shared in this book: global, holistic, transpartisan, sustainable, entrepreneurial, peaceful, innovative, and solution-oriented. It will feature the wisest and most courageous among us so that we take inspiration from their example and learn the principles that have helped them catalyze positive change.

Shift Media will also be designed so that people are not mere passive viewers but co-creators. When inspired by a particular leader or program, there will be opportunities to take action, generate media responses, form groups and social networks, and even organize campaigns. By bringing together community and grassroots mobilizing tools with inspired media, we will help move people into action and connect them with networks of like-minded citizens.

Our media strategy will eventually be paired with an effective system for training local leaders in creating positive evolutionary change in their communities. One way I see this taking form is through trainings built upon a highly distributed model, with curricula delivered at a distance to local training centers in bookstores, churches, town halls, yoga studios, YMCAs, and healing centers. Our distance learning courses will empower local learning communities that help people understand critical teachings and build leadership skills, as well as develop support systems for them to positively affect their local community. Because we humans are highly social animals, being a positive change agent is difficult without a network of social support. A well-designed training system will blend teleseminar and video content from top teachers, coaches, and facilitators, delivered mostly at a distance, with local circles of support, embodiment, and action. Content alone is not enough.

Part of the reason these leadership trainings need to be local is that there are simply not enough people who can afford to travel large distances to do personalized leadership trainings with top teachers. The trainings will eventually need to be affordable, accessible, and local.

In the system I'm envisioning, part of the function of The Shift Network will be to create a distribution system that has local Shift Centers where content from these leaders will be offered regularly and combined with personalized support. This will also create a business opportunity for entrepreneurs who run local centers, which might be as small as a single room in the back of a church or a side business for a bookstore, coffee shop, or YMCA. For the cost of a gym membership, people can join their local Shift Center and gain access to classes and trainings with top teachers, served up in daily workshop settings that allow members to engage in discussions, practice, and mutual support. Members might take an integral health course from Andrew Weil, a citizen activist class with Marianne Williamson, or a climate protection training with Al Gore, and then put those ideas into practice as a group. The local centers will also offer more personalized support in the form of coaching, spiritual direction, or healing work.

Over time, I believe that members of local centers will become the frontline leaders of positive change in their communities, as well as active participants in our evolving political scene. They can be inspired by Shift Media, empowered by Shift University courses online or at their local Shift Center, and supported in their leadership by circles of local allies. With such an infrastructure of support, everything from local politics to the community hospital to the local school board could benefit. A Shift participant might be part of local Solutions Councils or help create a publicly owned city bank or move forward large-scale renewable energy projects.

The truth is that we need evolution of our models at every level of our society and we need local leaders in each community, business, church, and school who are paving the way. The system I describe would allow a much broader cross section of America to engage with the brightest and most innovative leaders of our day, as well as form enduring and meaningful circles of local support that empower action. We have already launched hundreds of online learning programs as a stepping-stone to this longer-term vision, and I believe we are well en route to creating the larger vision, the kind of human architecture that can support an enduring evolution in our country.

31

World Campaign 2020

*The greatest revolution in our generation is that of human
beings, who, by changing the inner attitudes of their minds,
can change the outer aspects of their lives.*
—Marilyn Ferguson

IN THIS CHAPTER, I will share about a campaign that we are in
the early stages of developing to foster large-scale changes in the
years leading up to 2020, with a goal of culminating on the International Day of Peace—September 21, 2020. This campaign will
take the kinds of strategies that I've outlined throughout this book,
along with dozens more generated by other groups and alliances,
and build them toward a larger wave of positive change.

But first a bit of backstory. Before I launched The Shift Network, I created a Vision 2020 PowerPoint that offered a set of
strategies for how we could make this the turning point decade
for our planet. This roadmap informed the first five years of our
growth. And now, as I write in 2015, I remain convinced that we
can continue the momentum toward making this our turning point
time. We have already seen the rapid acceleration in adoption of
solar power, which hit an inflection point around 2012, with rates
of new solar installations soaring past all previous estimates (and

hopes). In recent years, we've seen a rapid rise of global women's movements, gay rights, electric car technologies, and more.

Our focus then becomes how to accelerate these changes by also accelerating a global shift in consciousness.

There's a power in focusing our collective attention on a timeline. Part of the reason 2020 offers such an auspicious date is that 20/20 is the term we use to describe perfect vision. What better time to shift our vision of the future on a massive scale than in 2020?

This impulse has evolved into what we are calling World Campaign 2020, which builds upon some of the same elements as a political campaign, only the goal is not to elect a person but to have a collective "election" of a new era of peace, sustainability, health, and prosperity. At the culminating moment on the International Day of Peace, we will have something like a collective "vote" for the future that we want to create, as hundreds of millions of people make pledges of global citizenship along with specific commitments for how they will make change in their own lives and communities. Between now and then, we will work to support groups, organizations, and larger movements to develop parallel campaigns that have bold change-the-world goals and that share the timeline of culminating on the International Day of Peace in 2020.

There are already quite a number of 2020 campaigns under way, from the Pope and top religious leaders calling for the end of all slavery by 2020 to a Village Banking 2020 campaign focused on getting basic banking to the two billion unbanked people in the world. World Campaign 2020 will act as an aggregator and enabler of these campaigns and empower them with media, outreach, and organizing tools to mobilize more effectively. It will provide a unifying timeline and infrastructure, as well as the inspiration for groups to create their own campaigns and be part of the larger movement.

What we've seen with political campaigns is that they are excellent at galvanizing massive amounts of engagement in a short period of time. By empowering parallel campaigns that target different areas of human suffering, from poverty to clean water to peacebuilding, we can make progress on the full spectrum of shifts that are required for us to make an overall planetary shift in our operating system.

Running these campaigns on parallel tracks but with a shared timeline will also be powerful because it will build a heightened sense of anticipation and collaboration as we near the end date, which is also the moment to celebrate our achievements collectively. That's why on the International Day of Peace in 2020, we are envisioning that it becomes a truly international event and that countries will declare a special holiday to mark a great moment of unification for humankind.

We also are envisioning the activation of the largest number of simultaneous peace concerts that has ever happened—festivals around the world to celebrate the music and culture of each country's unique contribution to a vibrant and thriving world. We are envisioning these separate concerts to be linked into a global wave of unification. Even if people are not able to participate in a live event, they will be able to watch on TV and mobile devices and catch feeds from around the world that showcase the culture and contribution of each nation. We are envisioning more than one billion people participating in this unifying day.

As part of the global celebration, we will invite participants to make a pledge to co-create this new era together. When people make this pledge, they will gain access to a year's worth of free daily content from top teachers, all designed to empower them in making their highest contribution and living their greatest life. We will also invite people to make a monthly financial pledge toward ending the major sufferings in the world. By getting millions of people to offer recurring monthly pledges to address some of the major challenges in our world, we would ensure more rapid progress.

Imagine further that on this historic day, all of the nations of the world commit to a daylong ceasefire as well as to aim for the lowest level of violence in history. In experiencing such a day, we would realize that it *is* possible for humanity to live peacefully together. We are also envisioning nations, states, cities, and organizations launching their own long-range visions for the world they wish to create. What if every country participating in the 2020 celebration also offered a media presentation of what their nation's vision for their fullest and most beautiful expression would be? To arrive at such a country vision would require the engagement of citizens and political leaders at multiple levels so that the vision becomes shared and a source of national pride.

I started seeding this concept of nations launching collective visions for 2050 a few years back when I was invited to speak at the World Cultural Forum in China. I suggested that China could lead the way for the world with a Vision 2050 that details its unique contribution and game plan for the creation of a peaceful, sustainable, healthy, and prosperous world. China is particularly well suited for such a vision as it is used to long planning cycles that are not dependent on short-term election victories. A few months later, I seeded the idea with the mayor of Duluth, Minnesota (my hometown), thinking it could be powerful on a local level as well.

Articulating a unique vision for a country or city can be incredibly powerful because it takes us beyond the swing between conservative and progressive poles of power and expands our collective vision of what is possible when we work together. It opens up a spirit of the possible. A longer time horizon gives us ample space to envision some major upgrades, which frees us from the usual cynicism and fear that nothing can truly change.

I also want to use World Campaign 2020 as a forum to build awareness and focus on the Sustainable Development Goals for 2030, which were ratified in 2015 by the leaders of 190 nations and are designed to end extreme poverty, fight inequality and injustice, and fix climate change. These seventeen goals (along with hundreds of sub-targets on more specific timelines) are quite bold in terms of alleviating poverty, addressing climate change, empowering women's education, and more. They chart a powerful course for our world to become peaceful, sustainable, and just. During the 2020 campaign, we can also commit to doing our part to fulfill the practical and detailed 2030 development goals, which will lead to real progress on all the major fronts we need to address. Critics say that these goals are unrealistic and overly ambitious in the absence of enforceable global laws, but there is a power in simply creating a shared vision and goals around which nations can align. The 2000 Millennium Development Goals were considered a moderate success by many, including the *Economist*.[1] Although not all eight goals and twenty-one sub-targets were reached from 2000, some key ones were, with progress on many others. The effort led to a reduction of abject poverty in the world by half and also cut in half the number of people without sustainable access to water and sanitation. These successes point to the fact that by opening to a commitment to making major progress, we open more to the methods of how to get there.

The seventeen Sustainable Development Goals are listed here. You can review them in much more detail online.[2] Each goal has a number of supportive targets that give specific timelines and markers of progress.

1. End poverty in all its forms everywhere

2. End hunger, achieve food security and improved nutrition, and promote sustainable agriculture

3. Ensure healthy lives and promote well-being for all at all ages

4. Ensure inclusive and quality education for all and promote lifelong learning

5. Achieve gender equality and empower all women and girls

6. Ensure access to water and sanitation for all

7. Ensure access to affordable, reliable, sustainable, and modern energy for all

8. Promote inclusive and sustainable economic growth, employment, and decent work for all

9. Build resilient infrastructure, promote sustainable industrialization, and foster innovation

10. Reduce inequality within and among countries

11. Make cities inclusive, safe, resilient, and sustainable

12. Ensure sustainable consumption and production patterns

13. Take urgent action to combat climate change and its impacts

14. Conserve and sustainably use the oceans, seas, and marine resources

15. Sustainably manage forests, combat desertification, halt and reverse land degradation, halt biodiversity loss

16. Promote just, peaceful, and inclusive societies

17. Revitalize the global partnership for sustainable development

It's quite a roadmap of goals that these 190 leaders have articulated. If we are able to achieve even a few of them, it is clear that we will be on track to living in a healthy, peaceful, sustainable, and prosperous world.

And lest we think these goals are impossible, the World Bank recently projected that in 2015, the number of people in poverty is expected to drop to 702 million, or 9.6 percent of the world's population, which is down from 902 million in 2012.[3] This is the first time in history that poverty will drop below 10 percent of the world's population and it puts us on track, provided we surmount the many hurdles ahead, with the goal of eradicating extreme poverty globally by 2030, which is remarkable.

World Campaign 2020 can offer a unifying timeline, a shared infrastructure, and a vision that many organizations and alliances can rally around in the short term, culminating with an "election day" global celebration that leads to a widespread commitment to do still bolder things in the decades to come. Imagine if we can get one billion people to participate in the day of global unification on September 21, 2020. What kind of impact might that have on our collective future? It's easy to be cynical and sometimes harder to let ourselves believe that major changes *are* possible and that we *can* do it. It's just a matter of focus and dedicated work.

If America takes a leadership role in creating the events and campaigns that build up to the planetary unification and commitment, it will be a powerful statement of our commitment to build a new American operating system that simultaneously helps transform the world.

32

The Call to Interdependence

In the past our glorious visions of the future—heaven, paradise, nirvana—
were thought to happen after death. The newer thought is that we do not
have to die to get there! We are not speaking here of life after death in some
mythical heaven, but life more abundant in real time in history. We are
discovering and participating in the next stage of our social evolution . . .
—Barbara Marx Hubbard

IN THE NEXT TWO CHAPTERS, I'm going to explore some of the biggest changes I see on the horizon as we begin to live into a fundamentally new, global operating system and make an enduring shift on our planet. These changes address the foundational levels upon which a truly global era will be built.

When constructing a new building, a great deal of planning is distilled into an architectural blueprint. The blueprint is the bridge between a vision and its tangible manifestation. Although it is relatively flimsy—at first only a few sheets of paper—a blueprint's power is vast because it provides the conceptual lines along which permanent structures will be laid down.

I bring this analogy up because I believe we are entering the phase of needing a new blueprint for both the United States and the world, one that adequately meets the environmental, political, economic, social, and global challenges of today. The creation and championing of such a blueprint can become a central aspect of the sacred evolutionary political movement we've been discussing.

The truth is that we now face deep, systemic challenges to the foundation of American democracy. We also live in a time when some of our primary challenges are now global challenges. There are parallels between the uncoordinated thirteen states in the 1780s and the chaotic network of nations today. As the most powerful nation on earth, America has an increasingly essential role to play in empowering the world's nations to act in unison to solve global problems.

What if we took the learnings from two centuries to forge a new and improved blueprint that thoughtfully addresses current power dynamics, the requirement for new checks and balances, and our relationship to international challenges, as well as provides enhanced ways for citizens to participate directly in government?

In parallel with history, the first step might be the creation of a unifying Declaration of Interdependence, signed by many nations, which could reflect the values and principles that underpin the worldview of America 7.0. This concept is not new; it was proposed in 1944 by Pulitzer Prize–winning historian and philosopher Will Durant, launched with a Hollywood gala, and began something of a small movement before being entered into the congressional record in 1949. Historian Henry Steele Commager made the second major attempt at such a declaration in 1975. Beyond that, a team of five from the David Suzuki Foundation launched a declaration at the 1992 Earth Summit in Rio de Janeiro, concluding poetically with, "At this turning point in our relationship with Earth, we work for an evolution: from dominance to partnership; from fragmentation to connection; from insecurity to interdependence."[1] Local governments, environmental groups, and various historians have been drawn to the concept, and a grassroots movement to turn September 1 (or perhaps September 11) into an international Interdependence Day has grown.

America is now too powerful to remain merely independent. Developmental psychologists have shown that the achievement of an independent self is an important step but not the ultimate destination of our growth. Independence is something normally achieved in one's early twenties, usually after a period of individuation from our family. Once we've made that developmental leap, though, the process isn't over. We must then start taking the needs of others as seriously as we do our own. Perhaps we start with a marriage partner, then children, a business, or a church. Our compassionate care expands to widening circles. Right action becomes defined less by what we want and more by what is good for the whole network—our family, our community, and our planet. We become interdependent.

The hallmark of mature adulthood is thus the capacity to think, feel, and act through the lens of interdependence. It is this kind of mature development that we now require to be institutionalized at the level of national principle. A worldview based on individualism fails in situations of systemic complexity because it can't take others' needs into adequate consideration. By advocating only for one's own interests rather than addressing the needs of the whole, individualism creates opposition and the use of aggression to assert the primacy of "our" needs. In turn, this feeds a climate of fear.

So, while the Declaration of Independence represented a momentous step in launching our country, it's no longer adequate for us to fixate on our independence when faced with twenty-first century global challenges. As the most powerful country in the world, we are called to step into the role of mature, global citizenship and act out of care for the whole rather than just our self-interest. The various attempts to create Declarations of Interdependence are all based in the same recognition that we have a higher and nobler destination.

What if America were to forge an enduring new pact, this time enrolling other countries of the world? This new statement would reflect and reinforce our interdependence with the entire planet and offer a sign that we are transitioning into a new relationship with our power. This could be done as a presidential act. Or such a national statement could also be achieved more organically out of a network of Declarations of Interdependence, from local city councils and schools to global NGOs. But its power and visibility would be greatly enhanced if it were eventually a presidential act that also enrolled Congress and other nations.

Such a signing would offer a decisive commitment to evolving the values of our country, honoring the independence on which we've built a strong country but committing to the still-higher principle of interdependence. This would undoubtedly be welcomed by the world and have foreign policy benefits as well.

While at first signing a Declaration of Interdependence would be more symbolic, commitments like this do have an impact over time and shift our relationships. A stronger commitment to interdependence would also open America to some of the deepest shifts of political systems that can truly transform life as we know it on planet earth, which I will explore in the next chapter.

33

Toward Global Governance

Today we must develop federal structures on a global level. We need a system of enforceable world law—a democratic federal world government—to deal with world problems.
—Walter Cronkite

I OPEN THIS CHAPTER with a quote from Walter Cronkite, long known as America's most trusted journalist, about the importance of evolving a system for global governance. This topic has often been marginalized by fear of a "New World Order," but some of the most respected leaders in history have seen such an evolution as essential for a peaceful and prosperous future, including Franklin Delano Roosevelt, Albert Einstein, Mahatma Gandhi, Václav Havel, and Mikhail Gorbachev.

Over the last hundred years, we've seen the emergence of many voluntary international accords and governing bodies, ranging from the United Nations to the International Criminal Court to the World Bank to Interpol to the World Trade Organization, all of which play a coordinating function between nations and help to stabilize international relationships. They each reflect the natural impulse to create a foundation for global culture that is just, harmonious, and lawful. But they are essentially voluntary accords between nation-states and are often paralyzed in their ability to act when faced with things like rogue nations, which often require more aggressive and expensive military interventions, typically by America and its allies. We do not yet have a way to directly elect representatives to address global challenges through a system of executive, legislative, and judicial bodies.

In this chapter, I offer a short exploration of this concept, even while recognizing that the details are beyond the scope of our space. Since it tends to be controversial, I'm simply asking you to try it on in a more exploratory fashion and open to the possibilities it offers.

I invite you to imagine for a moment a time in which we each have a vote in electing representatives to a World Congress of global problem-solvers. Imagine the best and brightest in the world serving on such a World Congress and that it is protected from the influence of lobbyists. Imagine this body is committed to ending war and terrorism permanently. Imagine that it sets a higher bar for protections against child labor, slavery, and human rights violations across the world. And finally, imagine that it allows us to successfully navigate economic and environmental crises with wisdom, setting standards that allow conscious capitalism to flourish in tandem with justice.

That is what I am quite sure is possible, if we take the time to thoughtfully design and eventually co-create a system of global governance with proper checks and balances. Most of the truly daunting problems facing humanity now reach beyond national borders. The solutions will require that our several hundred nations begin to act in greater synchrony than we have. Consider the following problems:

- War between nations and the refugees fleeing from them

- Global warming and other environmental challenges

- Terrorism

- Global financial market meltdowns

- Loose nukes

- Global pandemics

To adequately address these challenges, we need a trusted system of accountability, laws, and decision-making that go beyond the borders of a single nation. Otherwise, we have the rule of force on the global stage rather than law. The country with the biggest military then calls the shots in conflict situations, which can too often be for short-term self-interest rather than the good of the larger whole. In America, we have become accustomed to being the strongest military player and thus used to calling more of the shots, effectively becoming a kind of global police force, decision-maker, and arbiter of disputes. However, there are many challenges with this role in the long term, challenges that can imperil our economy and increase global warfare.

If America continues to occupy the role of global policing, it threatens to bankrupt our country and make us less competitive with other countries. We currently spend as much on our military ($610 billion) as the next seven biggest spenders combined (five of which are allies),[1] despite the fact that we are only 5 percent of the world's population. So long as there are rogue states and terrorist organizations and unstable despots who are rattling sabers and provoking wars, we'll have continued pressure to maintain and even increase that expenditure. Already, our defense budget has been a major contributor to an escalation of the national debt, with the wars in Iraq and Afghanistan bleeding our national treasury.

In places like the Middle East, where the United States has a very troubled history, it can be especially difficult for us to play any sort of a trusted intermediary or peacebuilding role. Instead, we tend to get involved in bloody, expensive, and lengthy engagements that fail to build functioning nations and often cause wholesale collapse. That's why shifting more of the global policing function to a global governing body, in addition to UN and international peacekeeping forces, will ultimately allow us to focus our resources on growing our economy and educating our people. Otherwise, we'll lag further behind countries that are spending the vast majority of their wealth on education, health care, and growing their economies. We'll slowly hollow out the strength of America.

I thus believe it is both practical and desirable for us to help create one more layer of organization beyond the nation-state that takes the form of a limited, democratic, and peaceful form of global governance, with appropriate checks on the extent of its power. We have city, county, state, and national governments. The existence of a state government does not invalidate or diminish the importance of county government. Nor does the national government negate the value or importance of state governments. Our Constitution allows for different levels of democratically elected leaders and balances the powers they wield. A healthy form of global governance is the natural last step on the road to a lawful, peaceful, and just world, one no longer held hostage by tyrants, rogue states, and the nearly constant threat of war or ecological collapse.

Global governance would have to be freely chosen and be sufficiently attractive to participating countries that they see participating as better than remaining outside, just as we've witnessed with the European Union, which has preserved many rights to nations while shifting some powers to transnational governance. While the European Union does have many legitimate critics and there are some real issues created by having a unified currency without unified economic decision-making, it has nonetheless paved the way to a stable, peaceful, and free continent, which is all the more remarkable when we consider the millennia of bloodshed that preceded it.

The United States of America is well suited to play a convening role in the development of global governance in the decades ahead for a number of reasons. First, we have long been committed to creating an ever more perfect union, an impulse that grew us from thirteen colonies with 2.5 million citizens into fifty states with more than 320 million citizens. We have a track record of scaling, evolving, and improving a democracy while addressing emergent issues and complexities. We also have experience in what it takes to balance national government with the power of states, which would be useful in designing the balance between global governance and nation-states. Obviously, we could not be the exclusive or sole leader in such an effort; but I am confident we can help find a pathway to make it successful.

I believe there will come a time when American political leaders will recognize that such a step is in both our best interest *and* the world's for the simple reason that we are currently playing some of the key roles of global governance in a way that is expensive, unwieldy, and ineffective because we are not seen as a sufficiently neutral actor, which ends up fanning the flames of more war, military buildup, and resentment. I believe we will eventually look soberly at the results and tire of the expense and the loss of life and determine that it is in our best interest to pave the way to a healthy form of global governance, which would allow us to take some of the economic, political, and even moral burdens off our backs while getting better results.

Now I do agree with the critics of such an idea that there are perils in creating global governance. Any kind of global governance will need to be quite limited in scope—certainly not more than 5 to 10 percent of the total decision-making political activity on the planet—as well as constitutionally protected from overreach into local, regional, or national affairs. The point is not to centralize more power than is absolutely necessary to achieve the goal of a peaceful and just world. When I talk about global governance, it's about finding *just* the right amount of oversight that is necessary to achieve a high-functioning global culture.

It is also wise to preserve the majority of political power for the most local level possible. Local government tends to be more accountable and accessible, which is why the relocalization movements have great value. The further removed someone is from us, the less influence we have over his or her decision-making process, and thus there is the very real danger that our needs and opinions will not be taken into account when making a decision or creating a law.

Even at our current scale of more than 320 million citizens, American democracy can feel remote. Our ability to directly influence our representatives and elected officials' opinions can appear limited. However, even with the challenges of scale, most of our elected officials in Washington do pay attention to the views of their constituents through tracking phone calls, emails, letters to the editor, and polls of key constituent groups. If we take the time to learn how to become effective citizen lobbyists, we can have a measurable impact on policy decisions, even in states with large populations.

This challenge is nonetheless significant on the level of global governance because each representative would be representing that many more people. Even if we assume seven hundred representatives in a World Congress, which is quite large for a legislative body, we're talking about an average representative representing over ten million people.

The real game changer on this front, though, is the Internet, which effectively makes the sharing of information instantaneous and free. In 2015, there are currently 3.2 billion Internet users, about 40 percent of earth's population.[2] Estimates are that we'll be in the 80 to 90 percent range by 2020. Since the creation of even early forms of global governance would happen well beyond 2020 even in an accelerated scenario, we can safely assume that virtually everyone in the world will be online by the time such a possibility becomes workable and desirable. That opens the door to a far more participatory form of global democracy.

What if every phone company were to agree to build an app for the purpose of providing real-time feedback for representatives in a World Congress? Let's say the Congress were deliberating about a bill and a representative were able to send a message to all ten million constituents via the app and each could respond with his or her opinion. Given the statistical nature of such things, within ten or fifteen minutes, representatives could have accurate data on the exact degree of support for a measure within their districts, which could then inform their work.

By designing a system of global governance to be supported by a participatory Internet platform, we could have a more direct, accountable, and immediate influence with a World Congress than we currently do with even our national government. A ubiquitous Internet is thus the technological foundation necessary for the creation of a system of global democracy that is sufficiently credible, accountable, and responsive to the real desires of citizens of planet earth.

For a system of global democracy to work well, we'd first need to establish a Constitution that makes it very clear what powers such a body has and does not have, as well as establish a rigorous code of conduct for representatives. The Constitution would preserve sufficient freedoms for member nation-states while also voluntarily centralizing some powers that are necessary to preserve global peace and ensure the rule of law. Beginning with a global Constitutional Convention, we could harvest exciting and innovative insights into the optimal forms of governance, based on several centuries of global experimentation. There are many people and groups that have already spent decades on such an effort under the banner of democratic world federalism.

Our times have emergent challenges that simply didn't exist in earlier centuries. As good as the framers of our own Constitution were, they did not have the benefit of several centuries of experience with democracy. A practical framework drawn up now might start with the principles that have been honed in our Constitution and new documents like the Earth Charter, and then be translated into a framework that could guide our next stage of collective evolution. It could offer upgraded protections as well as open new opportunities—a state-of-the-art framework for building an emerging global culture that respects the liberty and rights of every human being.

What can we learn about best practices from the many experiments in democracy around the world, many of which have higher rates of participation and satisfaction than our own? What can we glean from a serious study of the successes and failures in America? And how can we forge a new political structure that includes the wisdom of all voices? If we were to answer these questions in a coherent new way, giving shape to an emerging consciousness, we could lay down important guiding tracks for the next evolution of our world in a peaceful and prosperous direction.

The creation of global democracy will need to happen organically via the free choice of every nation that chooses to enter, much like what has occurred with the European Union. Member states would need to pass certain tests upon application, especially regarding the level of healthy, functioning democracy within their own borders, before being ratified as a participating member of what we might call the Global Federation of Democracies, which would also differentiate it from the United Nations, which includes all nations, whether they are democracies or not. Trying to bring a totalitarian state into full participation would undermine the functioning of that body. That's why global governance will likely need to build gradually, first through expanded regional unions and accords, then in the creation of more elected councils at the global level, then finally in a global federation with something like a World Congress. This sequential, step-by-step process of building also creates safety valves that prevent the development of anything that is oppressive or regressive.

The success of the European Union has led to other regional blocs beginning to form—a South American Union and an African Union, for example. These regional blocs have the power to honor the uniqueness of the cultures in that area while also coordinating actions between nations and reducing the propensity for those nations to go to war.

At the end of the day, I believe that it is part of America's destiny to use our superpower status to pave the way for a healthy but limited form of global democracy that can address many of our current global challenges. The 2014 Global Peace Index estimated the total global cost of violence at $14.3 trillion dollars, or about 13.4 percent of World GDP, of which 43 percent is attributed to military expenditures.[3] That number is staggering and sufficient motive to explore any pathway that can move us beyond the suffering, trauma, and loss associated with war and terrorism. And what is particularly shocking is that there has been a surge in the number of nations that are at the lowest level of stability, from three in 2008 to nine in 2015. In other words, the lower end of the scale is getting worse and worse, which is the zone that produces much of the terrorism we face.

An effective form of global democracy would eventually result in far less expensive and far more effective containment of violence around the world. Disputes between nations could eventually be settled lawfully in courts rather than at gunpoint. Grievances of weaker nations against powerful nations could lead to changes in global laws, thus providing more justice than if those powerful nations simply overwhelmed the weaker ones.

In the days after World War II, there was a tremendous surge of interest in world federalism and global citizenship. In 1948, a "world citizen" activist in Paris named Garry Davis asked world-citizenship advocates around the world to send letters of support to his public declaration of his world citizenship and in support of world government. The letters of solidarity filled an entire hotel, with multiple floors and hundreds of thousands of responses.[4]

However, as the memory waned of the destruction wrought by nation-states run amuck during World War II, so did some of the movement's power. Most people settled for the United Nations, an important advance but one that was nonetheless a non-democratic body without real lawmaking authority.

Our human nature is to resist change. A change as epochal as the creation of global governance will inevitably meet resistance from many quarters. The key is whether a problem big enough—World War III, economic meltdown, terrorism, or environmental catastrophe—can propel us past our resistance and fear to a truly effective and lasting solution.

The trajectory is clear: to expand our political unions toward regional blocks of nations and eventually a full global union of democracies. This will eventually create a path to a more peaceful, sustainable, healthy, and prosperous world that no longer squanders so many of our resources on the machinery of war or the waste that comes from hundreds of different countries having completely different rules and regulations in areas like trade.

If we take the task seriously and assemble the world's greatest experts with citizen representatives and cultural and political leaders, we can, over time, forge a workable system to address the world's most pressing problems collaboratively and move toward peaceful resolution of all disputes on a global scale. We simply need to open to it as a real and important avenue to ensure a peaceful, sustainable, and healthy future.

34

Fulfillment of America's Spiritual Mission

*Put your politics in one hand and Spirit in
the other, and fold them together.*
—Lorraine Canoe, Mohawk Indian leader

THE JOURNEY TOWARD FULFILLMENT of America's mission in service to all will not be complete, I believe, until we have helped end the long era of warfare between nations and ushered in a peaceful, sustainable, and prosperous planetary era.

At The Shift Network, we use the phrase "heaven on earth" to describe this more luminous possibility that represents the fulfillment of humanity's deepest dream of peace and opportunity for all. While it sounds lofty, the concept of heaven on earth can be quite practical as well. It is not about harps playing and angels singing; rather it's about bringing all our activities and societal structures into alignment with our most cherished sacred principles, ones that have been handed down through all our great religious and philosophical traditions. As this alignment happens, we can begin to make this world reflect a more enlightened way of being. The path has been clearly illuminated by teachers in every lineage, and it is up to us to learn how to walk it.

Part of why the founding documents of America have been so revered is that they emerged like holy texts, guided from above, but still written by the hands of men. They were a new template—a revelation of a pattern for how humans could bring their public affairs into greater alignment with universal truth. That is why they have been so effective; they are the natural expression of the evolution of human consciousness to express a more unified consciousness. And now we, as women and men, can do the same for our country and our world.

The lingering glow from the higher inspiration present at our founding continues to touch and inspire people everywhere. The challenge is recognizing that divine guidance is not only in the past but also right here in this moment. Right now. With you and with me. The very words I am typing are touched by a deeper Source. All of our most heartfelt and cherished dreams are also infused with sacred meaning. We are each guides to each other, collaborating with both friends and enemies in projects more vast than our human mind can comprehend.

I believe that the evolution of a truly sacred America and sacred world is something we and millions like us have been working on for a very, very long time. The next evolution of our country is neither sudden nor unexpected but as natural as a tree bearing succulent fruit at the end of a season of growth. If we listen only to today's news, it is easy to be seduced by surface appearances, which make it seem that these are dark and scary times—more apocalyptic than hopeful. Seen from a spiritual eye, though, I believe these times are setting the table for a long-awaited feast, a time of celebration during which the holiest visions we've inherited become practical, lived realities.

The deepest truth is that America has always been sacred, as have all other countries, cultures, and peoples of the world. There is nothing that is not sacred, nothing that is not woven with the threads of the Divine.

On an ultimate level, a sacred America is not something we need to achieve, although there are certainly major shifts that we've seen are important in every aspect of our society. Being sacred is something we just need to accept that we are. By bringing ourselves into alignment with our spiritual essence, we dissolve the angst and frustration that characterize so many people's lives. By bringing our country into greater alignment with sacred values and our higher mission, we can more easily discern right action. We can relax into a deep recognition of our oneness with all the peoples of the earth and live out our highest vision.

I have had many intuitions of the waves of change that are coming in the decades ahead. These waves may feel frightening for a time as old patterns are washed away, sometimes even violently. But I believe that the deeper evolution that they will bring is ultimately to be welcomed. When we have emerged from our time of collective growing pains, I believe we will stand in awe of what has been wrought on our planet, through all of our hands and all of our hearts. America's role in this coming shift will, I believe, prove essential and represent the fulfillment of our mission to serve humankind.

Conclusion

The best gift that we can give the world is a better America.
—Van Jones

WHILE THE SCOPE OF this book has been vast, addressing the higher mission for America as a whole and the complex evolution to get there, ultimately that mission is enacted person by person, step by step. Each of us carries the blueprints for a more evolved country in a more evolved version of ourselves. It is through our daily choices—to conserve precious resources, to engage our political process with wisdom, to love our families and our neighbors, to build conscious companies, and to offer our leadership for positive change—that the dream of a truly sacred America is made real.

As we each make a commitment to live our own sacred purpose, we spread our passion to others. We liberate ourselves to live more boldly and beautifully. We fill our small corner of the world with more grace. A well-lived life shines with more meaning as we become aligned with our creative Source and express our fulfillment through our unique service.

A sacred worldview respects every dimension of our lives. If we see that our bodies are sacred, we feed them healthy food, give them exercise, get adequate sleep, and care for them with practices that create radiant health. If we see our minds as sacred, we fill them with powerful ideas, inspired literature, moving media, and education that helps us perform at our best. If we see our families as sacred, we create a peaceful, loving, and safe sanctuary in which our children can explore. If we see our democracy as sacred, we take the time to become informed about our political decisions, express our convictions, organize for reforms, and support our representatives in finding a more enlightened path forward.

A sacred worldview leads us to have reverence for every aspect of life and see all people as expressions of the same divinity that transcends and includes all religious and spiritual expressions. This recognition in turn leads us to direct our creative gifts toward building a peaceful, sustainable, healthy, and prosperous world for all. That is the natural result of seeing our planet and all its inhabitants as worthy of reverence.

This book has explored my particular vision of the key elements that can help accelerate a shift toward this world in the decades ahead, with America playing a leading role. But there are more than seven billion visions for how to evolve our world, and all will be required. Each of us can create our specific pieces and link them with our neighbors and allies. That is how the beautiful mosaic of our future will be assembled.

I know in my heart that humanity has not yet reached the summit of our goodness, brilliance, or beauty. We often project those qualities into our idea of heaven, a place that we enter after we transition from the earth. The image of heaven is thus a beacon for us, a call toward our higher potential. But we need not wait. Making our planet a reflection of that image—a true heaven on earth—is a worthy mission. It is also not an instantaneous process but a journey that the human species has already been engaged in for millions of years. If earlier inhabitants of the planet were brought to today, certain aspects of our current world might resemble heaven, with godlike powers of transportation, energy, and communication. If we traveled a thousand years into the future, we might feel the same.

Heaven on earth thus may not be a final destination we attain but a compass setting to bring more wisdom, love, creativity, and joy into the world every day. We forge a better future by the hundreds of actions we each take: the food we eat, the words we choose, the clothes we wear, and the work that we do. In the end, the recipe is simple: we need to be the best person we can be and support others in doing the same. That is what it will take for more than 320 million Americans to realize our potential as a nation and stand in our greatness born of alignment with our divine Source that shines through all of us in our acts of love, service, and creative expression.

So join me in shaping the story of the next evolution of America by offering your own inspired story, written by the words and deeds of your life. In the end, that is how we will ultimately turn this page of history to a bright new day for America and for our world.

Acknowledgments

I offer my deepest gratitude for my beloved wife, partner, best friend, and co-creator of evolutionary change Devaa Haley Mitchell. Thank you for the many years of support, blessing, and fun in birthing this book and our lifework together. I love you deeply. Deep thanks as well to my parents, who have been my greatest champions. And a bow of gratitude to all whose brilliant thoughts, illumined teachings, and wise actions have inspired this book.

The development of this book was influenced, challenged, and honed by feedback from allies such as Saniel Bonder, Mark Satin, Byron Belitsos, John Steiner, Martin Rutte, Marianne Williamson, Mark Gerzon, Herb Hamsher, James O'Dea, and Anodea Judith. Together, you called forth a more complete picture, as well as alerted me to people and movements I would have otherwise neglected.

I am also deeply grateful for all the team members and teachers who have co-created The Shift Network with me and touched hundreds of thousands of lives with our experiment in creating a sacred company, particularly our leadership team of Jeffrey Kihn, Ben Hart, Alison Weeks, Philip Hellmich, Alison Marks, Sylvia Fry, Craig Kugel, and our cherished faculty including Andrew Harvey, James O'Dea, Barbara Marx Hubbard, Miranda Macpherson, Tim Kelley, Oscar Miro-Quesada, Sandra Ingerman, Gay and Katie Hendricks, Thomas Huebl, Lisa Schrader, Howard Martin, Deborah Rozman, Terry Patten, David Crow, Mirabai Starr,

Chief Phil Lane Jr., Patricia Ellsberg, Patricia Albere, Luisah Teish, Margaret Paul, Grandmother Flordemayo, Bill Bauman, Gabriel Nossovitch, George Kao, don Miguel Ruiz, Joan Borysenko, Lion Goodman, Carista Luminare, Corinne McLaughlin, Gordon Davidson, Shiva Rea, and Gangaji.

Finally, a deep bow of gratitude to those who shaped my growth and evolution, including Sadhvi Bhagawati, Swami Chidanand Saraswatiji, Michael Murphy, Stan Grof, and Dennis Kucinich.

Notes

Chapter 1

1. Paul H. Ray, "The Potential for a New, Emerging Culture in the US: Report on the 2008 American Values Survey," State of the World Forum, *http://www.wisdomuniversity.org/CCsReport2008SurveyV3.pdf*.

Chapter 2

1. See Van Jones's *The Green Collar Economy* for more exploration.

Chapter 3

1. Libby Kane, "This Psychology's Impressive Presentation Shows How Materialism Is Eroding Our Happiness," Business Insider, August 20, 2014, *http://www.businessinsider.com/materialism-eroding-happiness-2014-8?op=1*.

Chapter 4

1. Ray, "The Potential for a New, Emerging Culture."

Chapter 6

1. See Ezra Klein and Alvin Chang, "'Political Identity Is Fair Game for Hatred': How Republicans and Democrats Discriminate," Vox, December 7, 2015, *http://www.vox.com/ 2015/12/7/9790764/partisan-discrimination*.

Chapter 8

1. Mark Gerzon, *The Reunited States of America*, p. 186.

2. Jennifer Lentfer, "7 Things You May Not Know about US Foreign Assistance," Oxfam, April 1, 2014, *http://politicsofpoverty.oxfamamerica.org/ 2014/04/7-things-didnt-know-about-us-foreign-assistance/*.

Chapter 9

1. Russell Thornton, *American Indian Holocaust and Survival: A Population History since 1492* (Norman: University of Oklahoma Press, 1990), pp. 26–32.

2. You can still find the declaration and sign it at *www.declarationofcommitment.com*.

Chapter 10

1. Saki Knafo, "1 in 3 Black Males Will Go to Prison in Their Lifetime, Report Warns," *Huffington Post*, October 4, 2013, *http://www.huffingtonpost .com/2013/10/04/racial-disparities-criminal-justice_n_4045144.html*.

2. Eileen Patten and Jens Manuel Krogstad, "Black Child Poverty Rates Hold Steady, Drops among Other Groups," Pew Research, July 14, 2015, *http:// www.pewresearch.org/fact-tank/2015/07/14/black-child-poverty-rate-holds- steady-even-as-other-groups-see-declines/*.

3. See www.dreamcorps.org for links to all of Van Jones's initiatives.

4. Barrett A. Lee, John Iceland, and Gregory Sharp, "Racial and Ethnic Discovery Goes Local: Charting Change in American Communities over Three Decades," Department of Sociology and Population Research Institute, Pennsylvania State University, September 2012, *http://www.s4.brown.edu/ us2010/Data/Report/report08292012.pdf*.

Chapter 11

1. For an interview with Barbara Marx Hubbard that explores her concept of suprasex, among other topics, see: *http://www.som.org/ 3library/interviews/ hubbard.htm*.

2. Philip Bump, "The New Congress Is 80 Percent White, 80 Percent Male and 92 Percent Christian," *Washington Post*, January 5, 2015, *https:// www.washingtonpost.com/news/the-fix/wp/2015/01/05/the-new-congress-is- 80-percent-white-80-percent-male-and-92-percent-christian/*.

Chapter 13

1. Claire Cain Miller, "The Divorce Surge Is Over but the Myth Lives On," *New York Times*, December 2, 2014, *http://www.nytimes.com/2014/12/02/ upshot/the-divorce-surge-is-over-but-the-myth-lives-on.html?smid=fb-nytimes& smtyp=cur&bicmp=AD&bicmlukp=WT.mc_id&bicmst=1409232722000&b icmet=1419773522000&_r=4&abt=0002&abg=0*.

2. See "Child Poverty," National Center for Children in Poverty, *http:// www.nccp.org/topics/childpoverty.html*.

3. See "Births to Unmarried Women," Child Trends Data Bank, last updated December 2015, *http://www.childtrends.org/ ?indicators=births-to- unmarried-women*.

4. "Trends in Teen Pregnancy and Childbearing," US Department of Health & Human Services, last updated August 28, 2015, *http://www.hhs.gov/ash/oah/adolescent-health-topics/reproductive-health/teen-pregnancy/trends.html*.

5. Claire Cain Miller, "The Divorce Surge Is Over but the Myth Lives On."

6. For a good compilation, see "Children Divorce Statistics," *Children-and-Divorce.com, http://www.children-and-divorce.com/children-divorce-statistics.html*.

7. Ibid.

8. "Health Matters: How Life Decisions Affect Well-Being," *FamilyFacts.org/The Heritage Foundation, http://www.familyfacts.org/briefs/11/health-matters-how-life-decisions-affect-well-being*.

9. See *https://dovetaillearning.org/* for more details on this program.

10. See *http://www.qln.com/* for more details on this program.

11. See Emily Campbell, "Mindfulness in Education Research Highlights," Greater Good Science Center, September 16, 2014, *http://greatergood.berkeley.edu/article/item/mindfulness_in_education_research_highlights*.

12. See *http://passageworks.org/* for more details on this program.

13. See *http://www.challegeday.org* for more details on this program.

14. Tyler O'Neil, "A Divorce Costs Public $25,000 a Year, Says Reform Advocate," *Christian Post*, November 7, 2013, http://*www.christianpost.com/news/a-divorce-costs-public-25000-a-year-says-legal-reform-advocate-108299/*.

Chapter 14

1. For the full report, visit: *http://education-reimagined.org/*.

2. "The Art of Getting Opponents to 'We,'" David Bornstein, *New York Times*, November 3, 2015, *http://opinionator.blogs.nytimes.com/ 2015/11/03/the-art-of-getting-opponents-to-we/?_r=3*.

Chapter 15

1. "World's Top 5 Arms Exporters," UPI, November 17, 2015, *http://www.upi.com/News_Photos/Features/Worlds-Top-5-arms-exporters/3105/*.

2. Andy Kiersz, "The US Has Had the Western World's Worst Rate of Homicide for at Least 60 Years," *Business Insider*, November 12, 2014, *http://www.businessinsider.com/us-vs-western-homicide-rates-2014-11*.

3. Lauren E. Glaze and Danielle Kaeble, "Correctional Populations in the United States, 2013," Bureau of Justice Statistics, December 19, 2014, *http://www.bjs.gov/index.cfm?ty=pbdetail&iid=5177.*

Chapter 16
1. "US and World Population Clock," United States Census Bureau, *http://www.census.gov/popclock/.*

Chapter 18
1. Scott Peterson, "Inside the Mind of Iran's Khamenei," *Christian Science Monitor*, December 4, 2012, *http://www.csmonitor.com/World/Middle-East/2012/1204/Inside-the-mind-of-Iran-s-Khamenei-video.*

2. See *www.spiraldynamics.net* for more detailed analysis.

3. Jaweed Kaleem, "More than Half of Americans Have Unfavorable View of Islam, Poll Finds," *Huffington Post*, April 10, 2015, *http://www.huffingtonpost.com/2015/04/10/americans-islam-poll_n_7036574.html.*

4. "Islamic, Yet Integrated: Why Muslims Fare Better in America than in Europe," *Economist*, September 6, 2014, *http://www.economist.com/news/united-states/21615611-why-muslims-fare-better-america-europe-islamic-yet-integrated.*

5. Linda Mason, "What We Get Wrong about Iran," CNN, May 28, 2015, *http://www.cnn.com/2015/05/28/opinions/mason-iran-misunderstood/.*

6. See *http://cmbm.org/* for more information.

7. Check *www.kiva.org/* for the latest statistics.

Chapter 19
1. "Fact Sheet: US Reports Its 2025 Emissions Target to the UNFCCC," The White House, Office of the Press Secretary, March 31, 2015, *https://www.whitehouse.gov/the-press-office/2015/03/31/fact-sheet-us-reports-its-2025-emissions-target-unfccc.*

2. Bobby McGill, "Texas, California Lead Nation in Carbon Emissions," Climate Central, October 29, 2015, *http://www.climatecentral.org/news/carbon-emissions-spike-in-some-states-19615.*

Chapter 20

1. Ezra Klein, "10 Startling Facts about Global Wealth Inequality," *Washington Post*, January 22, 2014, *https://www.washingtonpost.com/news/wonk/wp/2014/01/22/10-startling-facts-about-global-wealth-inequality/*.

2. For more detailed information, see *http://www.finca.org/news/village-banking-2020/*.

Chapter 21

1. Silvia Ascarelli, "The $70,000 Minimum Wage Is Paying Off for That Seattle Company," MarketWatch, October 25, 2015, *http://www.marketwatch.com/story/the-70000-minimum-wage-is-paying-off-for-that-seattle-company-2015-10-25*.

2. Milton Moskowitz and Robert Levering, "The Best Employers in the US Say Their Greatest Tool Is Culture," *Fortune*, March 5, 2015, *http://fortune.com/2015/03/05/best-companies-greatest-tool-is-culture/*.

Chapter 22

1. "Beyond Greed and Scarcity," *YES! Magazine*, June 30, 1997, *http://www.yesmagazine.org/issues/money-print-your-own/beyond-greed-and-scarcity*.

2. Ellen Brown, "North Dakota's Economic 'Miracle'—It's Not Oil," *YES! Magazine*, August 31, 2011, *http://www.yesmagazine.org/ new-economy/the-north-dakota-miracle-not-all-about-oil*.

Chapter 26

1. Mark Gerzon, *The Reunited States of America*, p. 105.

2. Nate Silver, "As Swing Districts Dwindle, Can a House Divided Stand?" *New York Times*, December 27, 2012, *http://fivethirtyeight.blogs.nytimes.com/2012/12/27/as-swing-districts-dwindle-can-a-divided-house-stand/?_r=0*.

Chapter 28

1. George Lakoff, *Moral Politics: How Liberals and Conservatives Think* (Chicago: University of Chicago Press, 2002).

Chapter 29

1. See *http://www.emergeamerica.org* for more information.

Chapter 31

1. "The Good, the Bad and the Hideous," *Economist*, March 28, 2015, *http:// www.economist.com/news/international/21647316-which-mdgs-did-some-good-and-which-sdgs-might-work-good-bad-and-hideous.*

2. "Sustainable Development Goals," United Nations, *www.un.org/ sustainabledevelopment/sustainable-development-goals/.*

3. "World Bank Forecasts Global Poverty to Fall below 10% for First Time; Major Hurdles Remain in Goal to End Poverty by 2030," World Bank press release, October 4, 2015, *http://www.worldbank.org/en/news/press-release/2015/10/04/world-bank-forecasts-global-poverty-to-fall-below-10-for-first-time-major-hurdles-remain-in-goal-to-end-poverty-by-2030.*

Chapter 32

1. David Suzuki Foundation, "Declaration of Interdependence," *http:// www.davidsuzuki.org/about/declaration/.*

Chapter 33

1. Sarah Tully, "US Defense Spending vs. Global Defense Spending," Center for Arms Control and Non-Proliferation, May 14, 2015, *http:// armscontrolcenter.org/u-s-defense-spending-vs-global-defense-spending/.*

2. "ITC Facts and Figures—The World in 2015," report by ITU, official source for the United Nations, May 2015, *http://www.itu.int/ en/ITU-D/Statistics/ Pages/facts/default.aspx.*

3. "Global Peace Index 2015: Measuring Peace, Its Causes and Its Economic Value," report by Global Peace Index and Institute for Economics & Peace, p. 3, *http://static.visionofhumanity.org/sites/default/files/Global%20Peace%20 Index%20Report%202015_0.pdf.*

4. Garry Davis, *World Government, Ready or Not!* (Sorrento, ME: Juniper Ledge Publishing, 1984), p. 29.

Recommended Resources

Books

Tom Atlee, *The Tao of Democracy: Using Co-intelligence to Create a World That Works for All* (North Charleston, SC: Imprint Books/BookSurge, 2002).

Don Edward Beck and Christopher C. Cowan, *Spiral Dynamics: Mastering Values, Leadership, and Change* (Malden, MA: Blackwell Publishing, 1996).

Ellen Hodgson Brown, *Web of Debt: The Shocking Truth about Our Money System and How We Can Break Free* (Baton Rouge, LA: Third Millennium Press, 2007).

A. Lawrence Chickering and James S. Turner, *Voice of the People: The Transpartisan Imperative in American Life* (Goleta, CA: da Vinci Press, 2008).

David Gershon, *Social Change 2.0: A Blueprint for Reinventing Our World* (New York: High Point, 2009).

Mark Gerzon, *The Reunited States of America: How We Can Bridge the Partisan Divide* (Oakland, CA: Berrett-Koehler, forthcoming 2016).

Andrew Harvey, *The Hope: A Guide to Sacred Activism* (Carlsbad, CA: Hay House, 2009).

Paul Hawken, Amory Lovins, and L. Hunter Lovins, *Natural Capitalism: Creating the Next Industrial Revolution* (New York: Back Bay Books, 1999).

Barbara Marx Hubbard, *Conscious Evolution: Awakening the Power of Our Social Potential* (Novato, CA: New World Library, 1998).

Van Jones, *The Green Collar Economy: How One Solution Can Fix Our Two Biggest Problems* (New York: HarperOne, 2008).

Anodea Judith, *The Global Heart Awakens: Humanity's Rite of Passage from the Love of Power to the Power of Love* (San Rafael, CA: Shift Books, 2013).

Rachael Kessler, *The Soul of Education: Helping Students Find Connection, Compassion, and Character at School* (Alexandria, VA: Association for Supervision and Curriculum Development, 2000).

George Lakoff, *Moral Politics: How Liberals and Conservatives Think* (Chicago: University of Chicago Press, 2002).

Steve McIntosh, *Integral Consciousness and the Future of Evolution: How the Integral Worldview Is Transforming Politics, Culture and Spirituality* (St. Paul, MN: Paragon House, 2007).

Corinne McLaughlin and Gordon Davidson, *Spiritual Politics: Changing the World from the Inside Out* (New York: Ballantine Books, 1994).

James O'Dea, *The Conscious Activist: Where Activism Meets Mysticism* (London: Watkins, 2014).

James O'Dea, *Cultivating Peace: Becoming a 21st-Century Peace Ambassador* (San Rafael, CA: Shift Books, 2012).

John Perkins, *The New Confessions of an Economic Hit Man* (Oakland, CA: Berrett-Koehler, 2016).

Carter Phipps, *Evolutionaries: Unlocking the Spiritual and Cultural Potential of Science's Greatest Idea* (New York: Harper Perennial, 2012).

Paul H. Ray, *The Cultural Creatives: How 50 Million People Are Changing the World* (New York: Harmony Books, 2000).

Mark Satin, *New Age Politics: Our Only Real Alternative*, 40th anniversary edition (Camano Island, WA: Lorian Press, 2015).

Jerry Tetalman and Byron Belitsos, *One World Democracy: A Progressive Vision for Enforceable Global Law* (San Rafael, CA: Origin Press, 2005).

Marianne Williamson, *Healing the Soul of America: Reclaiming Our Voices as Spiritual Citizens* (New York: Touchstone, 1997).

Organizations

Abrahamic Reunion: *www.abrahamicreunion.org*

Alliance for Peacebuilding: *www.allianceforpeacebuilding.org*

Bridge Alliance: *www.bridgealliance.us*

Center for Mind-Body Medicine: *www.cmbm.org*

Center for Visionary Leadership: *www.visionarylead.org*

Challenge Day: *www.challengeday.org*

Club of Budapest: *www.clubofbudapest.org*

Conscious Capitalism: *www.consciouscapitalism.org*

Convergence Center for Policy Resolution: *www.convergencepolicy.org*

Democratic World Federalists: *www.dwfed.org*

Dovetail Learning: *www.dovetaillearning.org*

Ella Baker Center for Human Rights: *www.ellabakercenter.org*

Evolutionary Leaders: *www.evolutionaryleaders.net*

FINCA International: *www.finca.org*

Friends Committee on National Legislation: *www.fcnl.org*

HeartMath Institute: *www.heartmath.org*

Institute for Cultural Evolution: *www.culturalevolution.org*

Institute for Economics and Peace: *www.economicsandpeace.org*

Institute for Noetic Sciences: *www.noetic.org*

Kiva: *www.kiva.org*

Mankind Project: *www.mankindproject.org*

Network of Spiritual Progressives: *www.spiritualprogressives.org*

Nexus Global Youth Summit: *www.nexusyouthsummit.org*

Pachamama: *www.pachamama.org*

Parliament of the World's Religions: *www.parliamentofreligions.org*

PassageWorks Institute: *www.passageworks.org*

Pathways to Peace: *www.pathwaystopeace.org*

The Peace Alliance: *www.peacealliance.org*

Public Banking Institute: *www.publicbankinginstitute.org*

Quantum Learning Network: *www.qln.com*

Rebuild the Dream: *www.rebuildthedream.com*

RESULTS: *www.results.org*

Rocky Mountain Institute: *www.rmi.org*

Search for Common Ground: *www.sfcg.org*

Shared Hope International: *www.sharedhope.org*

The Shift Network: *www.theshiftnetwork.com*

Sister Giant: *www.sistergiant.com*

Social Venture Network: *www.svn.org*

Spiral Dynamics: *www.spiraldynamics.net*

Stir Fry Seminars: *www.stirfryseminars.com*

UN Sustainable Development Goals:
www.un.org/sustainabledevelopment/sustainable-development-goals/

Wolf PAC: *www.wolf-pac.com*

YES!: *www.yesworld.org*

Ygrene Energy Fund: *www.ygreneworks.com*

About the Author

STEPHEN DINAN IS THE founder and CEO of The Shift Network and a member of the Transformational Leadership Council and Evolutionary Leaders. The Shift Network was founded in 2010 and has served over 700,000 people worldwide, with customers in 140 countries. It delivers virtual summits, courses, and trainings featuring over 50 core faculty and 1,000 thought leaders in domains as diverse as spirituality, peace, holistic health, psychology, parenting, enlightened business, shamanism, Indigenous wisdom, and sustainability.

Stephen is a graduate of Stanford University (Human Biology) and the California Institute of Integral Studies (East-West Psychology). He helped create and directed the Esalen Institute's Center for Theory & Research, a think tank for leading scholars, researchers, and teachers to explore human potential frontiers. As the former director of membership and marketing at the Institute of Noetic Sciences, he was the driving force behind the Shift in Action program and the One Minute Shift media series.

He has been a featured speaker at the World Cultural Forum in China, the Alliance for a New Humanity in Costa Rica, Renovemos México in Mexico City, and the University of Cuenca in Ecuador, as well as many US conferences, events, radio programs, and online summits. He is also the author of *Radical Spirit*.

Stephen lives in San Rafael, California, with his beloved wife Devaa.

Hampton Roads Publishing Company

. . . for the evolving human spirit

Hampton Roads Publishing Company publishes
books on a variety of subjects, including
spirituality, health, and other related topics.

For a copy of our latest trade catalog, call (978) 465-0504 or visit
our distributor's website at *www.redwheelweiser.com*. You can also
sign up for our newsletter and special offers by going to
www.redwheelweiser.com/newsletter/.

More Praise for *Sacred America, Sacred World*

"*Sacred America, Sacred World* is a clarion call of hope. It conveys Stephen Dinan's spiritually inspired vision for America's political and cultural evolution. Steeped in the values of the left, he has come to understand an evolutionary vision of cultural change in which both Left and Right play enduring roles in the dialectic of progress, for which both must evolve. He offers an intimate, heartfelt confession of his sacred spiritual intuition in a way that speaks to the highest values of conservatives and radicals alike. Thoughtful, readable, original, and highly recommended!"

> —Terry Patten, founder of Bay Area Integral and author of *Integral Life Practice*

"*Sacred America, Sacred World* could not be more timely. It is profoundly courageous in penetrating the cloud of so-called 'realism' that keeps from dreaming a new dream for our country. It inspires and challenges each of us to look at our own beliefs and behavior that make us part of the problem rather than helping to birth the solutions. Stephen is also profoundly courageous in engaging with our greatest moral and political challenges—from income inequality and terrorism to racism and genocide. Both Stephen and his book meet these challenges with that all-too-rare combination of tough-mindedness and open heart."

> —Robert Gass, executive coach

"Dinan provides an alluring future vision for the new American dream! This is a call to move beyond labels or political affiliations in order to assemble as evolutionary citizens. *Sacred America, Sacred World* provides an open exploration of how to truly serve the collective whole in a way that works better for everybody."

> —Yanik Silver, author *Evolved Enterprise* and founder of Maverick1000

"I loved this book! Stephen Dinan is finally illuminating how politics can elevate America. This book takes us on a journey of hope and change, one not focused just on externals but on how we can unite our country as a whole to bring forth our best from within."

> —Sister Jenna, radio host and director of Brahma Kumaris, Washington, D.C.

"Reading *Sacred America, Sacred World* is like plugging into an evolutionary dynamo for the betterment of our precious country. It positively crackles with creativity, insight, unflinching analysis, and vision both sublime and practical. This 'Common Sense' from a fiercely patriotic, 21st-century Tom Paine is a must read for forward-thinking Americans of all parties and persuasions."

> —Saniel Bonder, founder of Waking Down in Mutuality™
> and author of *Healing the Spirit/Matter Split*

"Read *Sacred America, Sacred World*. Like breaking in new shoes, Dinan's prescription may be uncomfortable at first. But my prayer is that it can empower a seismic shift in perspective from focusing on one's own life to centering rightly on the good of our country and our world."

—Gayle S. Rose, CEO of EVS Corporation

"This book is simply beautiful, wise, and brilliantly conceived. It is a work of intellectual prowess, leavened with heart and wisdom that calls us to a new American Dream. It inspires hope for higher possibilities in our nation and the world."

—J. Manuel Herrera, Silicon Valley elected official

"We live in a sacred 'web of life,' with intricate connections that indigenous peoples have honored and respected for millennia. We are interdependent with everyone and everything. Stephen Dinan's call to embrace that interdependence in a new era of democracy is core to healing our country and our world. Thank you, Stephen, for sharing this vision for a sacred world and for this timely message to us all."

—Betsy Hall McKinney, founder and CEO of It's Time Network

"Stephen Dinan lays out a compelling vision for a nation and world with the political, economic, and social conditions needed to bring lasting peace and prosperity. And he advocates a clear path. *Sacred America, Sacred World* is a must-read for all those who yearn for a brighter tomorrow."

—Steve Farrell, worldwide executive director, Humanity's Team

"*Sacred America, Sacred World* gives us an inspiring Dream for the Future—and some very practical ways to get there. Stephen Dinan envisions a world that can work for everyone—and importantly so, because we're all in this together!"

—Olivia Hansen, President of Spiritual Life TV Channel,
and the Synthesis Foundation

"If the Founding Fathers could have written a book about the United States in contemporary times, this would be it."

—Walter Semkiw, MD, author of *Return of the Revolutionaries*